TO
BE
NEITHER
SEEN
NOR
HEARD

JESSIE RUTH
GASTON

written in
consultation
with
and
contributions
from
Faith A.K.N. Mulira

the life of Faith Alexandra Kamya Nasolo Mulira

Cover and interior images provided by Faith Mulira and are printed with permission.

www.kendallhunt.com
Send all inquiries to:
4050 Westmark Drive
Dubuque, IA 52004-1840

ISBN 978-0-7575-8766-5

Printed in the United States of America
10 9 8 7 6 5 4 3 2 1

This book is dedicated to:

My children: Sanyu Barnicoat, Mabel Herbert, Irene Lwamafa, and Damali Rita Osei
My informally adopted daughter: Sala Mirembe

My grandchildren: Derrick, Kofi, Kyomugisha, Dennis Jr.,
Sanyu, Kirabo, Kwame, Kojo, Nakasi, Cody, Tendo, and
Kukiriza-Suubi

And in loving memory of:
My son, Michael Sansa Mulira
My husband, Yona Mukasa Mulira
My father, Festus Mawanda Kibukamusoke
My mother, Yunia Nakasi
My stepmother, Elsie Nakayima Kibukamusoke

This book was authored and edited by Jessie Ruth Gaston, Ph.D. She is currently a professor in the History Department at California State University, Sacramento (CSUS). Dr. Gaston, originally from the state of Mississippi, received her B.A. in psychology at Occidental College in Los Angeles, and her Master's in African Studies and her Ph.D. in African, African American, and Middle Eastern History at the University of California, Los Angeles. She has received many awards and is the author of several publications. Dr. Gaston has traveled extensively in Africa and has served as the co-director of two Fulbright-Hays Seminars to Africa: one in Ghana in 2001 and the other in Rwanda in 2004. In June of 2007, Dr. Gaston was a member of a CSUS Educational Delegation to the Republic of South Africa. She serves on the Board for the Center for African Peace and Conflict Resolution at CSUS, and is also a member of the CSUS African Studies Coalition as well as a member of the nationwide African Studies Association. Dr. Gaston was the Director of the Cooper-Woodson College Enhancement Program in the Ethnic Studies Department at CSUS from August 2005 to May 2007. She was recently selected for the sixty-fifth edition of *Marquis Who's Who in America, 2011*. Dr. Gaston is a very supportive member of South Sacramento Christian Center and the proud mother of Sanyu Ruth Kentugga Mulira.

CONTENTS

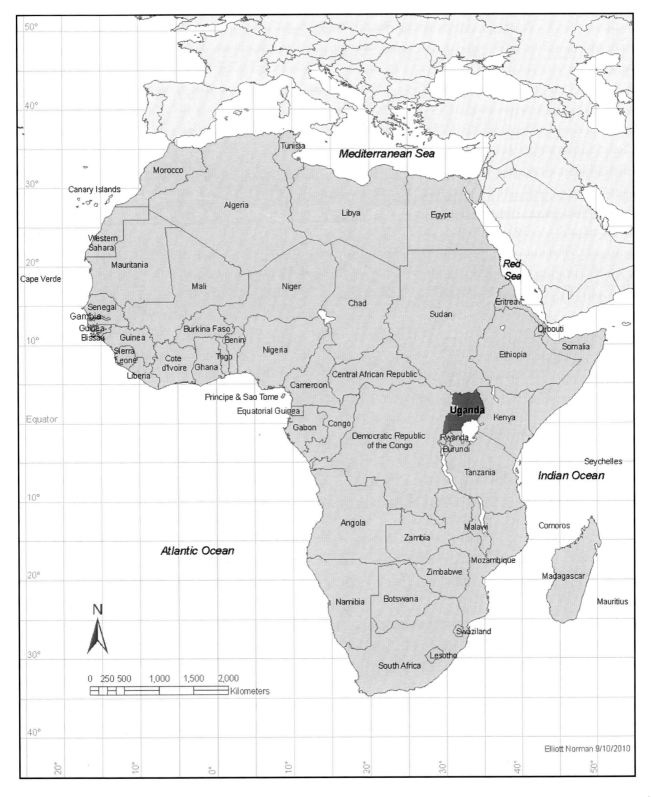

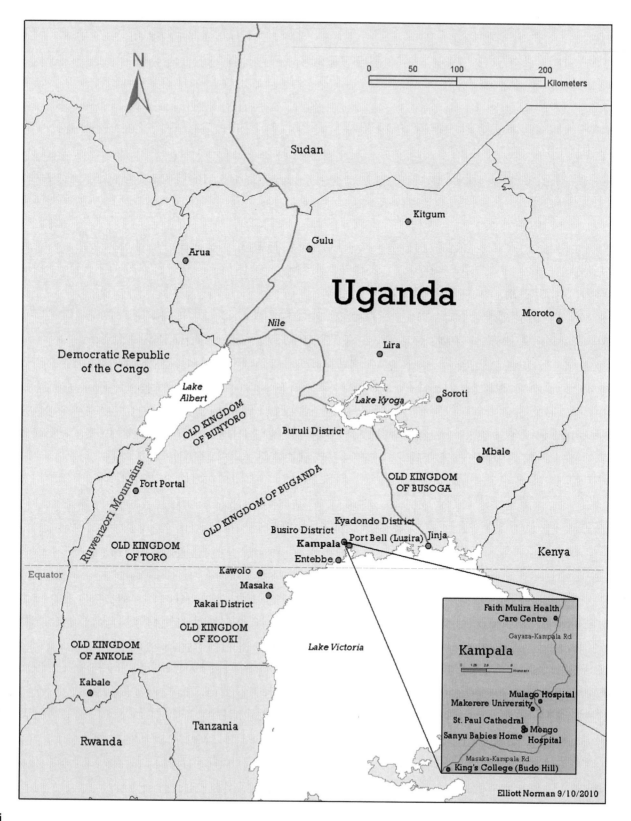

It gives me great pleasure to be associated with the efforts of this remarkable lady, Faith Mulira—although I am more inclined to call her Faith Kibukamusoke, the name I associate with the family—whom I have known for more than fifty-eight years. Some fifty-eight years ago is when I entered the most famous school in Uganda: King's College Budo.

To be sure, there were four of us from one extended family in Ankole, in western Uganda. There were also families that had children in both the six (Budo Junior) primary classes and in the six secondary classes. You could recognize them by their family names. But, without a doubt, the Kibukamusoke family was one of those families who had generously populated Budo. This came out clearly at roll call, where we were called in alphabetical order, the family name coming before the first (Christian) name. In the senior school alone, you had such names as *Douglas, Shemmie, Roscoe, John, Rhona*, and *Paul* that were all preceded by *Kibukamusoke*. Quite impressive, eh?

Shemmie was in the commercial class, parallel to my academic class. We attended the same class and used similar textbooks for English and geography. Douglas, who was two years ahead of me, lived in the same "South Africa House" with Paul and me. Paul, who was two classes behind me, also joined the commercial classes when I was in my final year.

Two fathers were famous for their interest in their children's education. One was Rwot (Chief) Erachito Okech of Acholi, who lived hundreds of miles away but always took the opportunity to come over to Budo just to see how his children were doing in class. He had three children at Budo: Daudi Ochieng, who was in his final year together with Douglas when I arrived at Budo; Martin Aliker, who was my classmate; and last, Janet Arach, who lived in the girls' house across the "equator," and who was a class or two behind us. Mr. Okech must have had several other children in other schools, because at one time, his family was reputed to be the most educated in East Africa!

The other one was Festo Kibukamusoke, Faith's father. It was said that he would come over on Saturdays to give written tests to his children until they passed the stage he himself had attained. It was also said that he would ask for the school reports of his children as soon as they arrived home for holidays, before he even greeted them, and to have rewarded them (in pocket-money amounts) according to their grades. There was the other reported extreme! While at school, all children had a more or less equal share of food, but it was different at the Kibukamusoke home, where the measure of food for each child was equated to their performance in class. Thus, it was said that poor performers returned to school rather emaciated. No wonder, then, that all Kibukamusokes did well in class. In any case, if it was true that the Okech family was the most educated in East Africa, the Kibukamusoke family was certainly very close to the top.

As Faith indicates in her book, Festo Kibukamusoke, who perceptively defied tradition by educating his daughter privately, and at great expense, was certainly draconian in the administration of his household, the reason why many of the boys would or could have resented and disliked their father. His outlook was what the fastidious called "mad." Indeed, there was a newspaper article in which he was said to have sued his wife in court for "spreading rumors" that he was "mad." Nevertheless, there is no doubt that he meant well for his children, for whom he sought, identified, and placed in the best and most expensive school of those days. May the Almighty bless his soul!

Faith Mulira is a remarkable woman. The story of her great achievements and services to the human race, at home and abroad, to the young and abandoned, and to the aged and infirm is a story of selfless ambition and marvelous perseverance. Of great faith and trust in God, overcoming seemingly insurmountable obstacles (for which she has won enviable accolades), including residing in Uganda during the "reigns" of

Idi Amin and single-handedly taking care of her family, including building them a house, her story is one of extraordinary success. Triumphing over conservative opposition to the progress of women and the prudish ridicule of their potential attributes, Faith Mulira has rightly earned her place among Uganda's prominent daughters, wives, mothers, and grandmothers.

Again, I must say that I feel honored for being considered competent to write this foreword to her life story.

F. D. R. Gureme
Kampala, Uganda
July 29, 2002

As an adult, I have always enjoyed sharing stories of my life with others. I have found that comparing my growing-up experiences with those of other cultures and generations to be not only beneficial but also eye-opening experiences. As far back as the 1960s, a very dear friend, William (whose actual name is Professor William Senteza Kajubi), suggested that I consider putting my life story in print. He was also a longtime friend of my brothers and had gone to King's College Budo at the same time. William had heard the story of my growing-up experiences over and over again, and he was the first person to inspire me. As an adult, he taught in the Department of Education at Makerere University and was later appointed as the vice chancellor of Makerere University. He went on to become the vice chancellor of Nkumba University, and he served in that position until he retired about two years ago in 2008. Over the years, he would consistently ask me, "How far have you gotten on the book?" However, in the beginning, I gave little thought to his idea. Then, some time later, I had the opportunity to care for a very nice elderly American lady, Anne Malley, who continuously asked me what it was like growing up in Africa. She, like William, would always listen attentively to my every word. At times, she also shared her stories and experiences. One day, she told me about her mother and her sister-in-law, who was the first female attorney in Hartford, Connecticut. She would also talk about her precious children, whom I had the opportunity to meet while she was one of my health-care clients. I was always amazed at how such an elderly person, who was already past ninety years old when I first met her, was able to provide such beautifully detailed descriptions of her yesterdays.

Anne, with her great sense of humor, not only became a mentor for me, but also inspired me to think of my life experiences as worthy to be shared. One day, as we were comparing and sharing episodes of our lives, Anne said,

> Faith, your stories and experiences of your childhood are quite unique. Why don't you write a book? I think it will be very interesting to read. Come on, do it! Do it quick! We can write a page together every day you come. You know, we people in this country [United States], do not know what you people [Africans] are going through growing up in Africa. We take things for granted and when we [Americans] see you, we do not have a clue that you have gone through hardships. So, write a book and let me know when it gets published. I will be the first person to buy a copy.

So, I started with her encouragement to write down and to compile notes on my life. And every time I arrived at her home, she would ask, "How far have you gotten?" That was quite a number of years ago. Anne died in October 2000 at the age of ninety-four. I also became well-acquainted with her children, especially her son, Professor James Malley, who joined his mother in encouraging me to write a book on my life experiences. Professor Malley is an Associate Professor Emeritus of Counseling and Family Therapy at Central Connecticut State University. He retired in 2006 but continues to teach part-time. In addition, he is the Chair of the Connecticut Partnership for Sustainability Education, Inc. Another client, Gioconda Di'Mella, also loved listening to my stories. She was my client for some three and a half years between 1996 and 2000. I took care of her until she was strong enough to require less caregiving assistance. We became very good friends. We laughed, joked, danced, and mourned together. Mrs. Di'Mella also promised to buy one of the first copies of my future book. She has also passed.

Over the years, I have had wonderful individuals—like Shupan Abraham, a dear friend of my daughter Mabel who lives in Georgia—who extended their services to me. For a short period of time, she did a lot of typing for me as I was writing down some of my initial memories. Then, after Shupan, Mr. F. D. R. Gureme, who had a reputation as a good writer, embarked on editing what Shupan had typed. He not only read over what Shupan had typed, but did some additional typing of some of my notes. This was a long time ago, and both Shupan and Gureme tried their best to assist me, but they did not have the time. Gureme had attended King's College Budo with several of my siblings. However, he was also a dear family friend with firsthand knowledge of what we went through growing up in our family, because he was the only person who used to stop by our home on the way from school when we were younger. He is the close family friend who wrote the foreword for this book way back in 2002 in hopes that it would one day be published. I am so grateful for his very kind words and the flair with which he expressed himself.

The individual to whom I am most grateful for the completion of my life story is Dr. Jessie Ruth Gaston. Dr. Gaston, who is also my former daughter-in-law, is the author and editor of this biography. She helped me tremendously by putting bits and pieces of information from me into an organized format. Sometimes, the data came from previously typed paragraphs or notes. At other times, the information came from my responses to questions she sent to me via e-mail, or from my responses given to her over the telephone, or handwritten responses sent through the postal service. Dr. Gaston's expertise in the field of African history was very much appreciated, because she was able to enrich and embellish my life story with historical incidents and events of historical significance. This contribution will enable you, the reader, to have a greater understanding of my life experiences and the surrounding factors that impacted my life. Dr. Gaston also secured the publisher for this book, and I am elated that Kendall Hunt Publishing Company saw the value in publishing my life story.

I would also like to extend my gratitude to the following persons who have had a positive impact on my life, either by encouraging me to put my life in print or by simply having a profound impact on the life I have lived thus far. First of all, I would like to thank Dr. Hebe Welbourne, who was instrumental in getting me into nursing school and the job at Sanyu Babies Home (SBH). Second, I would like to recognize Dr. Jan Johnston, a pediatrician, who was my employment supervisor in 1980 while I was taking care of her mother-in-law, Helen Johnston, for three and a half years in Newington, Connecticut. Helen was also my first client in the United States, and I worked with her until she passed. Dr. Johnston also encouraged me to get a certificate in gerontology in order that I might be able not only to increase my knowledge as a caregiver, but also to earn a better wage.

I want to acknowledge my mother, Yunia Nakasi, for her relentless love that always encouraged me to be patient regardless of the situation. She gave me the strength and a hope for a brighter future. I miss her dearly. I want to thank my father, "Festo very Baada," for his hidden love and his desire to educate me despite cultural and family resistance. He succeeded in providing me with a foundation and a personality constitution that helped to make me strong, independent, success-driven, and the loving person I grew up to be. I would also like to acknowledge my stepmother Elsie, who took care of me from the time I was five years old. She was only about seventeen when she married my father, who was about thirteen years older. For her to take care of her new husband's three children from another woman at such an early age is to be admired. Then, to my late and former husband, Yona, I would like to acknowledge his tremendous love, patience, and courage that helped me to become a mature adult and mother. He was a good man and a wonderful father, but his life was cut short because of his illness. To my children (Sanyu, Michael, Mabel, Irene, and Damali), to my informally adopted daughter (Sala Mirembe), and to my grandchildren (Derrick, Kofi, Kyomugisha, Kwame, Sanyu, Dennis Jr., Kirabo, Kojo, Nakasi, Cody, Tendo, and Kukiriza-Suubi), I hope that each of you will find my life story interesting and informative. I would like to thank two grandchildren in particular, Sanyu Ruth Kentugga Mulira, for assisting in the selection and scanning of the photographs as well as helping in the formatting mechanics of this book and Kyomugisha for assisting in proofreading the text. I would also like to thank a dear and longtime friend of my author, Mr. Glenn Fleming (a mechanical engineer), for his assistance in scanning and the electronic filing of the photographs. A special appreciation goes to my five children. My daughters Mabel and Damali served as my oral historians. They provided me with so many of the details of our shared experiences and events as a family. Damali, in particular, remembered explicit details on what they experienced living with their father while I was attending the University of Swansea in the United Kingdom and later when I was working in Kenya. My daughter Mabel, but especially Sanyu and Irene, took time out of their busy lives to type up my responses to Dr. Gaston's questions. Sanyu and Dr. Gaston must also be recognized for all of their heartfelt efforts in getting the photo and model releases as well as the contributor's agreement forms signed and returned to Kendall Hunt Publishing Company. I want to also thank my late son Michael for writing the best business plan for one of my largest and most cherished life projects, the Masooli Project.

Last, I would like to recognize and to thank the Almighty God to whom I give praise for my long journey in life. I have been so blessed by him. It is only through his grace that I am strengthened. I believe there are a lot of people who grew up experiencing the kind of life I did. But, with hope, determination, and a willingness to learn, they can provide themselves a path to a brighter future. Do not lose hope. God will extend his blessings to whoever asks and truly trust in him. We have a saying in Uganda, "*Katonda kyaterekera omunaku tekivunda,*" meaning that God has quite a lot of blessings for each and every one, no matter who they are. So, I would suggest that you read this book from the beginning to the end. Enjoy it. To God be the glory.

The country of Uganda, which is roughly 91,100 square miles, is a relatively small East African country. It is predominantly a Christian nation, and it shares borders with five other African countries, including the Democratic Republic of the Congo, the Sudan, Kenya, Tanzania, and Rwanda. Uganda consists of two major climatic zones, the plains of the Northeast and the Southern highlands. To the south of Uganda is Lake Victoria, which is the source of the longest river in the world, the Nile River. This particular River flows for more than 4,000 miles, starting in Jinja, situated about fifty miles east of Kampala, the capital city of Uganda, and eventually enters into the Mediterranean Sea through Egypt.

The southern part of Uganda is graced with lush, green, tropical rain-forest landscapes. The average altitude of 4,000 feet above sea level and the proximity to Lake Victoria combine to produce one of the most comfortable climates in the world. When it rains, it can pour for thirty minutes at one time, and then the sun will usually burst out defiantly and shine all day as if it had never rained. In Western Uganda, the Ruwenzori Mountains rise up and penetrate the clouds with uncommon ease, grace, and beauty, providing breathtaking views of natural phenomena. However, in Northern Uganda, the tropical rain forests give way to more arid terrain.

When the British first arrived in this region in the nineteenth century, they found four societies/kingdoms in the Southern highlands that were so well organized that it was not necessary to colonize their inhabitants formally. The inhabitants of these four kingdoms—Buganda, Bunyoro, Ankole, and Toro—not only spoke related Bantu languages, but their organized societies predated the arrival of any European visitor by hundreds of years, who only arrived in sizeable numbers in the 1860s. One of these societies, the Kingdom of Buganda, had set up such a highly advanced administrative infrastructure headed by the **Kabaka** (king), that the Europeans likened it to the feudal monarchies of medieval Europe.

The predominant ethnic groups to the northeast, including the Acholi, Langi, Karamojong, Iteso, Madi, and Kakwa peoples, lacked the political heritage of hierarchical state building in favor of less stately organized societies. They were also more likely to be cattle-keeping pastoralists than agriculturalists. In addition, these Nilotic groups in the Northeast were linguistically separated from those of the Southern highlands. In the early 1890s, when the British decided to cement their claim over this East African region that they had acquired at the Berlin Conference in 1884 and 1885, which was organized to settle the scramble for Africa, they ignored the cultural, linguistic, and political differences between the peoples of the Northeast and those of the Southern highlands. Consequently, the two geographical regions, the Southern highlands and the Northeast area, were united under one colonial political entity, the Uganda Protectorate. To do this, the British are said to have created a series of laws and treaties, in addition to using gimmicks and pretexts, like protecting the Protestant faith and trying to stop a civil war from breaking out between the different religious affiliations in this region.

After the British had established themselves, they integrated the ruling class of the Southern highlands, especially those of Buganda, into a system of indirect rule, the policy of ruling through the traditional kings and chiefs while maintaining the ultimate control. It is said by many that the British had some difficulty in pronouncing the word *Buganda*, so they resolved the issue by dropping the "B" at the beginning of the word and calling the region *Uganda*. There are other local oral traditions that provide different origins of the word "Uganda." For example, one tradition claims that the name *Uganda* was initially the Swahili version of *Buganda*. Arabs and Swahili peoples from the East African coast had entered this region in the 1830s as traders. Another very interesting oral tradition contends that the name is linked to the first king of the Buganda Kingdom, whose personal name was *Uganda*.

Regardless of its origins, the term was, after 1894, used to refer to the entire British Protectorate and not just the Kingdom of Buganda. Under colonial rule, the two regions developed separately. Some of the people in the Southern highlands benefited economically from the colonial cash-cropping economy. This was especially true for the Buganda ruling class, who benefited financially from cotton production. They also benefited educationally because there were many from this group who had the funds to send their children to the Western-style missionary schools. Their opportunity to benefit from colonial rule can also be associated with the fact that the headquarters of the colonial government was situated in close proximity to what might be referred to as the "traditional" lands of the Baganda. Their influence is reflected today in the fact that even though the official language is English, the lingua franca is Luganda. This also means that Luganda has succeeded in supplanting the former lingua franca, Kiswahili, which is spoken today by fewer Ugandans. Presently, the Baganda ethnic group is also one of the largest—if not the largest—in population.

During the colonial period, there was also a growing class of Asian entrepreneurs who played a very important role in the local economy. And they tended to fare better in the colonial economy than most Africans, especially those in the Northeast region. Since the colonial government neglected the Northeast region and its populations, the people were forced to become migrant workers in the South in order to earn money to pay the colonially imposed taxes. Furthermore, they were targeted as recruits to serve in the colonial security forces. This situation was to be the root for much of the conflict during the initial years of Uganda's independence, which occurred in 1962.

Today, the present government estimates the population to be from 28 to 30 million people and the country's gross domestic product to be less than 10 billion dollars a year. This of course means that Uganda is certainly one of the poorest countries in the world. This condition is largely the result of the twenty years between 1966 and 1986, when Uganda endured the very repressive military regimes of Apollo Milton Obote (1962–71 and 1980–85) and that of Idi Amin Dada (1971–79). Uganda is also considered the first African country south of the Sahara Desert to have succeeded in overthrowing a military government through a popular revolution, led by a small group of freedom fighters. This took place in 1986. It is unfortunate that Uganda is often characterized by its darkest hour even though on a visit in 1945 Winston Churchill described the country as the "Pearl of Africa." In reality, Uganda is a country of decent, talented, hardworking, and resilient people who have demonstrated their true character by what they did before and after the turbulent twenty years.

Since the defeat of the military regime in 1986, Uganda has embarked on the enormous task of rebuilding the crippled infrastructure and economy left behind by the military regimes. There has been significant progress over the last twenty or so years, and the economy has grown at an impressive average rate. Unfortunately, the growth has been more in terms of rebuilding the shattered economy rather than building prosperity. Various tenets of modern democracy have been restored to the country under the present leadership of the Honorable President Yoweri Kaguta Museveni, a hero leader of the 1986 nationalist movement.

Michael Sansa Mulira
Business Plan for the Masooli Project, 2007
Jessie Ruth Gaston, Ph.D., 2010

Chapter 1

MY BEGINNINGS AND MY PARENTS' TRADITIONAL MARRIAGE

I am the second of eighteen children, which includes two who died in infancy, and the only girl child among the first six children. I grew up under the strict moral and social codes and rules of my father in a local society that believed children in general were to be seen and not heard. However, for the first female child in particular, she was to be neither seen nor heard. My father, Festus Mawanda Kibukamusoke, was born on March 1, 1896, at Nakasongola in Buruli District, situated thirty-five miles from Kampala, the capital of Uganda located in East Africa. In fact, he was born two months after his father, my grandfather, was killed in a civil war when he stepped forward to protect his chief. So, my grandmother single-handedly reared my father until he was seven years old. However, when his mother remarried, she left him to grow up and be raised in the household of the same chief his father had died protecting. This particular chief already had several wives and at least forty children of his own. At this time in history, polygamous marriages were widely accepted by the majority of the people. And this was especially true for those who followed a traditional lifestyle. It was actually a custom of the Baganda for traditional village chiefs to have many wives. This particular chief had a main house where he lived and other smaller houses to accommodate his wives that surrounded his yard, all of which formed a "homestead." Within this polygamous household, my father was treated well. It is also important to note that this particular chief operated in the service of the kings of the Buganda Kingdom. Such chiefs were referred to as the *Ssaza chiefs* and were always the Kabaka's head rulers stationed in different parts of the Buganda Kingdom. Under British colonialism, they were put on the colonial payroll. Some of them also received monetary as well as sociopolitical benefits and incentives from the Kabaka's local traditional government.

As my father's foster parent, this chief took great care of him. He was sent to a local school, where he excelled in his studies. As a result of his academic success, the chief enrolled him in the most prestigious high school in Uganda, King's College Budo, where he obtained a full academic scholarship from the colonial government, which financed his six years of high school. This school was founded by British missionaries and was established on the British model. Under this British-based educational system during the early stages of colonialism, the high-school level was the highest academic level for Africans in Uganda. So, after high school, my father was hired to teach in one of the middle schools, where he worked until he was hired in the civil-service department as an accountant's clerk in Kampala at the Department of Revenue. At this time, my father was the only Ugandan who was working with the British colonials as a cashier in this office.

My father often returned to the chief's homestead for visits, especially during school semester breaks and summer vacations. Unbeknownst to the chief, my father had also developed romantic feelings towards one of the chief's beautiful ladies. Apparently, the feelings were mutual, because on one of his later visits, the lady, Yunia, sneaked off and eloped with my father. She left her four children (two boys and two girls by the chief) with the chief, which was expected in our patrilineal society. They stayed together and, according to customary law, were considered married. They had three children, two sons and one daughter. That daughter, born August 7, 1924, was me. My older brother Douglas was born in 1922 and my younger brother Shemmie was born in 1926. A midwife delivered each of us at the hospital. There were no traditional birth rituals performed, since my father never believed or observed such traditional customs.

According to some oral traditions, my family through my father's bloodline descended from members of the royal family in Bunyoro in the Hoima District. The Bunyoro Kingdom dates back many hundreds of years. We never got this confirmed in writing or any complete oral verification; however, each of my siblings and I carry royal surnames that are the surnames of the Baganda royal family. My mother, Yunia Nakasi, was born at Kitagobwa in Kyadondo District around 1893. Unlike my father, my mother had very little if any formal education. However, I do remember that she was able to read and write, but not very well. My mother was not a princess, nor was she a mere housewife of the chief in Buruli District, who was also a *Ssaza chief* in the Buganda traditional government. She was the **Kabejja**, leader of the other wives, and was considered the most beloved wife of the chief. According to my mother, she and my father were both physically attracted to each other. He was attracted to her beauty, and she was attracted to his very handsome, masculine physique. My mother also contended that she had grown tired of the many responsibilities associated with her position as the leader of the chief's wives. In other words, she might have needed a break from her life of responsibilities. It really does seem that my mother's union with my father was only between the two of them.

My father took on a second wife several years before I was born. Moreover, he decided to legitimize this marriage with a church marriage ceremony in 1922, two years before my birth. His second wife, Elsie Nakayima Kibukamusoke, was born on December 13,1906. None of her roots are really known to me, but she could have been from Buswa in the Busiro District, where some of her relatives live today. She was only seventeen when she married my father, who was almost thirty years old. I do not know how Elsie and my father met, nor do I know whether there was a bridal price/wealth given. Less than two years after my brother Shemmie was born, my father sent my mother away. I still remember that morning. I had gotten up early to find my mother in tears. My father had told her to leave the house and never to return or visit us. I was about five years old. To this day, I do not know why she had to go. We children were also told not to have contact with her or to talk to her people, who lived at Kitagobwa about fifteen miles from Kampala. In reality, we did not know how to contact her, because she had gone back to her former husband, the chief at Nakasongola, some thirty-five miles away. With my mother gone, we three were left in the care of my father's young, inexperienced, but charming, kind, and beautiful young bride. The real challenge was my brother Shemmie, who had many medical problems. In fact, it was thought in local terms that he was going to be lame/physically challenged in his legs. So, I was assigned to help take care of him, but I too was very young. It took Shemmie more than three years to crawl and to stand on his two feet alone. He grew up with many scars on his knees from multiple surgeries, but he proved not to be physically challenged. I vaguely recall how he would cry all the time, and I felt so sad for him. I truly believed that he was missing the love and tenderness of our mother. I used to think that if only our mother could come back, things would be all right. So began the story of my life growing up.

My father and his new bride had a total of fifteen children together, including the two who died in infancy. One child died at the age of one; he had an opening in his trachea. The second was stillborn. The living children, including my direct siblings and me, numbered sixteen—nine boys and seven daughters, with me being the eldest girl of my father. We were named Douglas, Faith, Roscoe, Shemmie, John, Paul, Rhona, Joseph, Daniel, Mary, Ndiwoza, Abraham, Moses, Evelyn, Florence, and Maria. All of Elsie's children were born in the hospital. Together, we lived in a three-room house that was built by my father on land that he had purchased in Kampala. The house had two bedrooms and one large living/dining room combination. We had only two acres around the house and some more land belonging to the government was connected to our land; since nobody was using it for anything, we used this land to grow food. I usually slept at my grandmother's, that is, Elsie's mother, who lived with us. However, she had a separate small, thatched cottage where she stayed. Based on cultural tradition, she ate her meals alone in her cottage and we, the grandchildren, took turns sitting with her at mealtimes—only in the evenings. She could never sit and eat at the same table as her son-in-law because of cultural taboos. Her husband had died before Elsie married my father. Some of Elsie's relatives used to visit us, and we kids were always happy to get visitors, since our father seldom took us to visit any of our relatives. So, as the oldest daughter, I slept in the cottage with Elsie's mother, while the rest of my siblings managed to squeeze themselves in that one large bedroom. They had to roll up their mattresses during the day to create room to move around. Looking back, I find it hard to figure out how we managed. Our kitchen was an outside room because we used firewood for all the cooking. Today, it sounds tough, but it never had a negative impact on us when we were young, except for the times when thieves broke into the kitchen and ran away with our chickens. This actually happened numerous times, so my father on occasion had to strengthen the locking device on the door to make it harder for the thieves to break in.

Figure 1: My father's house, where all sixteen children once lived and grew up.

Chapter 2

MY FATHER, HIS NEW WIFE, AND US CHILDREN

My father was a perfectionist and wanted all of his children to be like him. Whenever he told you to do something, he expected you to do it without any questions or reservation. He always told us what he thought and instructed us to accept his version regardless of anybody else's opinion. In fact, he was a no-nonsense kind of guy and was not usually affected by what other people might say. For example, during the time that I grew up, women never rode bicycles. However, many times when he sent me out to deliver something or to take a letter to his friends in the neighborhood or to pick up something from the store, he ordered me to ride a bicycle to wherever he sent me. I was always uncomfortable, but I would take one of the boy's bicycles because we had none for the girls. Bicycles were for the men and boys. So, I used to get on the bike if there was nobody on the street looking and then, I would jump off once I saw somebody on the street coming toward me. Then, I would get back on only after the person had passed me. This getting on and off the bicycle caused my trip to be longer than usual, and I always wondered why my father never asked me why it took me so long to go and come. At times, my father's no-nonsense attitude caused others to develop negative views of him. For example, he rode his bicycle to work five days a week, but he seldom took the time to greet anybody on the way to work and back home. He was always punctual leaving and returning home, so he passed the same people all the time.

Some of our neighbors created nicknames to refer to my father. One of the most popular nicknames, "Festo, very Baada," had been given to him while he was in school. The name "Festo" is really a biblical name in one of Paul's Epistles in the King James Version of the Christian Bible. In the Bible, Festo is a good guy. However, his classmates gave it a negative connotation in reference to my father. People my father's age would also tease him, stating that he always looked so serious because he had so many children to take care of. He disliked it, but he never really seemed to care what they thought of him. Whenever he did speak to our neighbors, he usually spoke in English, and when those who could not understand English tried to speak to him in Luganda, their language, he replied to them in English. So there were many who thought him to be very arrogant, and therefore called him names other than his real name in an attempt to annoy him.

In many respects, my father was very much influenced by the British and their ways of life and thinking. In fact, he behaved and thought more like a British man in a black man's skin. It is really amazing how his behavior, living style, and manner of speaking were so English influenced. However, there was one exception: He had a large number of children. It was his Westernized mindset that made it very difficult to mix or interact easily with other Africans around us. It also led to my father prohibiting us from associating on a more personal level with our neighbors. In addition, we seldom visited other relatives or friends while growing up. Even in the naming of his sixteen children, he made sure that we each had an English or Christian first name. Believe it or not, my father had selected our names from a book of Western and religious names before we were even born. For example, my full given name is Faith Alexandra Kamya Nasolo Kibukamusoke, but I dropped my father's name when I got married, which is thoroughly acceptable in my culture. I have always been grateful that he saw fit to name me after his mother, whose name was Kamya. I felt very special and honored being the only girl out of seven daughters to be my grandmother's namesake.

His Western ways were also obvious in his refusing to obey certain food taboos of his ethnic group. Each Baganda clan is distinguished by a totemic restriction. My father's clan is represented by the deer. This means, then, that my fifteen siblings and I also belong to his clan, being that our society is patrilineal. My mother's clan, on the other hand, is associated with a small bush, "**Akatinvuma**," while a type of fish called the mamba represented my stepmother Elsie's clan. In families where the clan is represented by an edible animal, the clan members are forbidden to partake in the meat of that animal. The same goes for clans associated with a plant. Such plants or foods become taboo for the members of the clan. However, in my father's house, we were allowed to eat everything, whether it was clan-associated or not, including the deer, the mamba, and the leaves of the **Akatinvuma** bush. Ironically, though, my father did enforce the tradition of his mother-in-law not being allowed to eat at the same table as her son-in-law.

This totemic system was originally established to strengthen the relationship of clan members in the areas of mutual assistance and defense, whenever necessary. This system was also designed to regulate the social life of the community, especially where marriages were concern. Marriages were to be exogamous, that is, outside of one's descent group. However, once people, including my father, began to assimilate Western ways, they started to let go of many of their traditional practices. Such changes also spread into sacred cultural practices. For example, people from the same clan were forbidden to intermarry, but now some of the parents of the intended partners did not take the clan's designation to be that serious. My father's acceptance of the European ways of doing things did not mean that he was fully accepted by them as a full human being, or that they welcomed him in their homes. To the British, he simply had been more or less successfully colonized and was therefore not a threat.

In actuality, he had very few real friends who visited him regularly. When we were growing up, these friends were always in his age group, in the same socioeconomic group, and usually in similar professions. He especially had friendly relations with some of the teachers at the various schools where my siblings later attended. And, of course, he had also attended the most prestigious of them all, King's College Budo, and still had contacts there. Whenever these few friends visited with us, we had peaceful and relaxed evenings, because my father would cancel our homework sessions. We children would always keep our fingers crossed that the visitors would stay until dinner. On such occasions, it was obvious that father yearned for their warm companionship and lively conversations. Oh, how they would talk and laugh! My father would seem so lighthearted during these visits. Boy, he was never that way with us. Normally, he was not an openly friendly person. In fact, as for us children, we cannot remember any time when our father really gave us a genuine smile. If he did smile at all, it was a grin, but it looked like a very fake smile and only lasted for a few seconds. We children never responded to his smile for fear of it being an incorrect response.

Even though our father was very strict, we had lots of fun when there was no school for my siblings and our father was at work. On those days, we would generally have seven hours to, peacefully or wildly, do the nicest things or the most mischievous things. The seven hours were counted from 8:00 A.M., when my father left the house, until 4:45 P.M., when he was expected to return. On such days, we would be especially quiet at dinner. There would be nothing to talk about because we had done all our talking, laughing, yelling, and general craziness before my father returned from work. He simply thought we were following his rules about being quiet during meals. The weekends were the longest days we had. With our father's "quiet rule," there was no noise to be heard over the weekends in his house when he was home.

Oh, but we had so much fun when he was at work and we were home. We children usually played well together. But we never had any relaxed time with our father in which we held a normal conversation. Our time with him was always formal or study time. So, we felt proud among ourselves whenever we thought we had outwitted him. For instance, we used to help ourselves to a spoonful of Ovaltine (a chocolate powder drink by Nestlé) each time one of us was told to go and fetch something from the pantry. Ovaltine does not dissolve that easily in the mouth. In fact, when we put a heaped spoon of dry Ovaltine in our mouths, it was almost impossible to speak for a while. So, before it dissolved, Mama Elsie would be calling the person she sent in the pantry and wondering what was keeping him or her in the pantry so long. And, in the process of putting the Ovaltine in our mouths so hastily, of course it got sprinkled either on the counter or on the floor, where it used to form a sticky surface on the pantry floor or counter. I believe that Mama Elsie realized why the floor and counter were sometimes very sticky, but she never admitted to our father that we were responsible. No way! For my brothers and sisters, it became something to laugh about, since we knew the secret of why the Ovaltine jar emptied so quickly. We took pleasure in thinking that we had gotten something over on our parents.

My stepmother Elsie understood that we children found it sometimes difficult to live up to my father's perfectionist expectations and rigidity. So, Elsie, being the caring person that she was, would often try and find a way to let us know that she loved us unconditionally. For example, knowing the possible punishment, she never told our father of her suspicion about us sneaking and eating the Ovaltine. Even though Elsie would never publically disagree with my father, she was not above doing what she felt was right in such a way as not to challenge his authority or tradition. When my father sent my mother away, he did so with strict orders, forbidding her ever to visit us again. This was not a decision made by Elsie. In fact, Elsie would allow my mother to visit on occasion when he was not home. Yunia would creep through the bushes in the garden and make a signal that she was around, and then my stepmother would let her know if it was okay for her to come and visit her children. Elsie, most likely guided by motherly instincts and realizing that my father's whipping cane would not be used on her, would allow my mother to stay and visit for some time. And what was even more astonishing was the fact that none of the other children ever mentioned my mother's visits to our father. We all knew the possible consequences for blatant disobedience to one of father's decisions.

My father always emphasized how we should keep together as brothers and sisters. He bought us books to read that stressed the importance of brothers and sisters envisioning themselves as a bundle of sticks that are tied so tight that no outsiders would be able to break them up. He preached this to us so many times. He also taught us to be strong in the Lord and his power to protect us. He not only made us learn but to recite regularly Psalm 121 from the King James Version, which reads:

> I will lift up my eyes to the hills
> From whence comes my help?
> My help comes from the Lord,
> Who made heaven and earth.
>
> He will not allow your foot to be moved.
> He who keeps you will not slumber.
> Behold, He who keeps Israel
> Shall neither slumber nor sleep.
>
> The Lord is your keeper;
> The Lord is your shade at your right hand.
> The sun shall not strike you by day,
> Nor the moon by night,
>
> The Lord shall preserve you from all evil,
> He shall preserve your soul.
> The Lord shall preserve your going out and your coming in
> From this time forth, and even forever more.

My father emphasized the Lord's protection just as much as he stressed how we should always keep together as brothers and sisters. He made sure that we read those books that stressed the importance of the brother-and-sister bond. Unfortunately, we children never developed that "oneness" our father used to preach to us about when we were small. As children, we all played a lot together, but as we grew up, we all went our separate ways. Luckily, each of us has been successful in many of our personal pursuits.

Ironically, as much as he sacrificed and did for us to help us grow up into useful citizens, we never realized or felt his love at the time. In fact, there were times when we did not think that he had a grain of love for us. None of us sixteen children remembered ever receiving a hug from our father, nor did any of us children ever desire to give him a hug. In the real sense, maybe hugging was not part of the cultural mores or was not seen as a necessary act of love. We lived by his strict orders all the time and we saw him more as a figure of authority than anything else. He always wanted us to be busy doing something serious while he was home as opposed to holding regular conversations with him. So, when he was home on some Saturdays, we all played not only outdoor games like cricket, baseball, and football, but also what my father referred to as more "organized" and "sophisticated" board games that were imported from Europe, like Ludo, Snakes, Chess, or Meccano, which consists of building blocks and construction pieces. Meccano was very mechanical. With these blocks and construction pieces, we learned how to build or rather construct miniature structures like those used by men who built highways and bridges. We learned how to put the pieces together also to build cars, houses, and bridges using these blocks. Ludo is a game where you shake a tube and throw down a small cube from the tube that has numbers on it. When the number comes up, you move the cube to that number on the board. The first person that gets a total score of one hundred is the winner. The Snakes game is similar to Ludo. You move your cube following the number at the bottom of the snake figure to the end of the snake. When the top of the snake is at one hundred, you are a winner. If it is any other number, you add up the numbers you already have. At least one evening during the weekdays, we also had to read a book or practice our knitting or sewing whenever my father was home. In other words, our father kept us occupied. And, even in our games, father emphasized the importance of being perfect in whatever we did.

This was the same type of attitude my father exhibited toward our performance of our regular household chores and family expectations. My father, as a notorious perfectionist, pushed his children to follow in his footsteps. He would always tell us what he thought regardless of the opinion of anyone else. In fact, referring to the opinions of others to prove a point with my father was not accepted at my father's place. For example, his household was very organized, and we children had regular chores and daily routines that were not to be questioned or avoided. We had to take turns serving the food, helping to prepare the meals, washing the dishes, sweeping the floors, and doing the laundry. We had to also do our father's laundry in turn, boys and girls alike. We would press his clothes and lay them out for him every morning. It was mandatory that we wash our clothes and iron every single outfit we wore. Laundry for everyone had to be done on Saturday, and all the clothes had to be done for the entire week. There was nothing like wearing pants or dress outfits without ironing them first. In those days, most private homes did not have electricity. In fact, electricity was largely found in the houses of British colonial officers. So, we used charcoal irons. The top of the iron flipped open for the hot coals to be placed inside and then fastened down. Believe it or not, those irons were very efficient.

There was one chore that my father reserved for the boys. That was fetching water from the spring. My brothers used to have to carry the water buckets on their head. My father said that he would not let his daughters do this type of heavy work because it would cause them to have a difficult delivery when it came to childbearing. He believed that that kind of work would make the pelvic bones go out of alignment and make for complications in the future. As I grew up, I came to understand the real reason. Most of the spring wells were located in isolated areas, so most parents never allowed their daughters to go to fetch water from the far-off spring wells as a way of protecting them from harm, including rape.

Our daily routine was somewhat automatic. After waking up early in the morning, we made our beds or rolled up our mattresses and then made breakfast in turn. Before leaving the house in the morning and going to bed at night, there was always time dedicated to the reading of scripture; usually, one scripture was read from the Old Testament and another from the New Testament, followed by a prayer from the prayer book and a hymn of anyone's choice. As each child learned to read, he or she took his or her turn in the reading of scripture and praying from the prayer book. They also took turns saying the prayer at mealtime. My father made sure that we each had a copy of the prayer book and our own personal copy of the Bible. So, there were eighteen Bibles and eighteen prayer books in our home. The actual breakfast was prepared in turn, too, boys and girls alike. It usually consisted of a small bowl of cereal or hot maize porridge, a slice of bread with butter, and, occasionally, a slice of sweet potato instead of bread, and a nicely blended cup of tea with milk. At times, we also had a spoonful of Ovaltine added to our half-cup of milk. We especially enjoyed it and looked forward to that half-cup of chocolate milk. What we didn't enjoy was the daily spoonful of cod-liver oil given to us for medicinal purposes.

Such above mentioned chores were expected of us regardless of any visitors at our home. Our well-organized and well-run household, coupled with the sometime well-established guests who visited our home, caused some neighbors to think that we were a well-to-do family. On the outside, we looked well-fed, clean, and prosperous. However, the neighbors did not know what was actually going on within our family, because we were never allowed to mix with them or their children. Ours was a close-knit kind of isolated family. Not having enough

Figure 2: Family portrait with my father, Elsie, twelve of my siblings, my future husband, and me, taken on November 29, 1945.

food was never a problem at my father's house. We were fortunate that there were all kinds of vegetables and fruits grown on our land. However, we were never allowed to waste food. If we happened to put too much food on our plate, we were forced to finish eating it with a swipe from my father's cane on our backs, which was designed to remind us to put less on our plates at the next meal.

So there was never any food left on our plates, because we learned to put less on them. We were so fortunate that food was never a problem until the boys grew up and needed a lot more food, but by then, they had already gone. We were well-fed and reasonably well-dressed, but we were not rich. As I mentioned earlier, all of us boys and girls had to learn how to knit and sew, and we made some of our own clothing, including our own sweaters. In fact, the older children had to knit a sweater for themselves as well as one for a younger sibling. I now understand that our father was teaching us how having certain skills can help you to become more self-sufficient and less dependent on someone else. In addition, it was far cheaper for us to knit our own sweaters than for our father to buy sixteen new sweaters.

Chapter 3

A FORMAL EDUCATION FOR MY BROTHERS, BUT NOT FOR ME

In our society, when I was growing up, there was little to no importance placed on formally educating the girls. I really desired to attend school, and I envied my brothers and later my sisters who were sent to school one by one as they reached school age. (In fact, my sisters Norah, Florence, and Maria went to Gayaza, while Rhona and Evelyn attended King's College Budo.) I was so unhappy because they were given an opportunity to learn to read and write, and to learn about new things, while I was left home to do housework and to babysit my younger siblings. So, I would constantly ask myself, why was I singled out? What had I done to be denied the opportunity for a formal education? The reasons were never explained to me, nor were the reasons that my father sent my mother away ever explained to me. In fact, it remains a mystery.

The preference given to males continues to be practiced in many African societies, especially in patrilineal family structures. In such a system, inheritance is through the father's side of the family. It also means that the children are said to belong to the father's side of the family. So, if there is a divorce, the children usually go to the father's home or to his relatives' homes. There are some African societies where matrilineal family structures are the norm, and in such families, inheritance is through the mother's side of the family. So, if there is a divorce, the children are viewed as belonging to the mother's side of the family. However, even in matrilineal family structures, it is usually the oldest brother or male cousin, in the absence of a "real" brother of the mother, who exercises the paternal rights and assumes the majority responsibility for the children.

From time to time, I indirectly made my educational desires known to my father. But my official request to go to school was made by my stepmother, Elsie, because it was not easy for me actually to approach him for anything that required my going away from home. Gosh, I was too afraid to ask him directly. My dream became a reality in 1932 when he enrolled me in one of the best schools in the country, King's College Budo Primary School. I was eight years old when my father enrolled me as a student, and I was one of the first twelve girls to be enrolled in that institution. Most of the teachers were Africans but a few were British. I loved the school, but I cannot remember what subjects I liked most. I liked our school uniforms, which were red with white trimmings. I also liked very much that I was living away from home, but I never did like the meals at school. Transportation to and from school was always a challenge, but we were fortunate that some of our friends' fathers would sometimes give us a ride to school. I am sure that school fees were expensive; this was one of the reasons that some members of my extended family did not think it was necessary to spend so much money educating a girl who would end up getting married to take care of her husband and kids. They wanted to make sure that the girls, and especially the eldest, were at home learning how to cook while helping their mothers care for any younger brothers and sisters.

The first Western-type schools in Uganda were established starting in the 1890s by European missionaries of various denominations. For example, the Protestant Church established King's College Budo and Gayaza High School, while the Catholic White Fathers established St. Mary's College Kisubi and the Mill Hill Mission from London established Namilyango College. King's College Budo, which continues to be a very prestigious coeducational boarding school, was established in March of 1906. Its name is a reflection of its geographical location and cultural affiliation. It is situated on Budo Hill in Busiro County, Wakiso District, in Central Uganda, off the

Kampala-Masaka Highway, less than nine miles southwest of the capital city of Kampala. Ethnically, this region is largely populated by the Baganda people. And situated on Budo Hill is also the cultural coronation site referred to as *Naggalabi Budo*, where the kings—Kabakas—of the Kingdom of Buganda were and continue to be enthroned in a traditional ceremony. In addition to King's College Budo and Budo Primary School, there is also situated, at present, a coed nonresidential Budo Senior Secondary Day School. King's College Budo is still one of the best academic institutions in Uganda, and it remains very expensive. According to local oral and written sources, and probably some English and mission documents as well, it was also the school where the traditional rulers, like the kings of Buganda, starting with Captain Sir Daudi Chwa II (the thirty-fourth Kabaka, who reigned from 1887 to 1939), and their princes attended. Today, the majority of the citizens in top positions in the country have probably sat in classes at Budo at some time in their lives. It is important to note that the British colonial government established in the early 1890s did not participate in the establishment of a formal education system until the 1920s. And, even then, they only gave grants and assisted schools that were already established. Even as late as 1950, the colonial government operated only three of the fifty secondary schools for Africans in Uganda. There were three others that were privately owned. All of the remaining schools were established by missionary groups.

As mentioned earlier, many of my father's relatives did not support my father's decision to enroll me in a formal school. They would bombard him with their verbal disapproval and openly complained how he was wasting too much money on educating a girl when there were "so many boys" needing an education. One relative went as far as to say that the boys would be of more value to him in the future. Another said, "Gosh! What are you going to do with an educated daughter? She is not going to take care of you." There was yet another relative who voiced to my father, "Your daughter can get her education here [at home] by doing the housework. She does not need more than that." My father, hampered, hindered, and constrained by social norms, a cultural environment that gave preference to males, and pressure from his relatives, took me out of Budo after only one semester. I was hurt, heartbroken, and really devastated. Afterward, I was made to stay at home while the boys went off to school not only to experience other worlds through their studies, but also to improve their opportunities for better lives. So, for a while, my father succumbed to their view that it would be foolish to spend money to educate a girl, since I would eventually leave his household to get married, taking my education with me. Nevertheless, these same relatives never voiced any resistance to my father's sending my sisters to be formally educated when they reached the appropriate age.

My father's relatives were unaware that he had not been fully convinced that I should not be formally educated. To my joy, he spoke to some of his European civil-servant co-workers and friends at the Department of Revenue, where he worked as a cashier, about the conflict with his relatives over educating his oldest daughter. Even though he was the only African hired to work in his position, he was very content with his situation. To even discuss issues from his private life with non-Africans implies that he must have felt comfortable with his European co-workers, especially when he hardly said good morning to fellow Africans in route to work. These fellow co-workers suggested that he purchase some English Linguaphone records that could teach me to speak English. The records came in sets of twelve records per set. The cost of the records was enormous at the time, but he put a few shillings aside each month until he was able to buy the records at the cost of about 300 Ugandan shillings—when he only earned 333 Ugandan shillings a month, which equated to about 165 U.S. dollars. It was a miracle that my father was able to do this with so many children to feed at home on his meager salary. The decision to purchase the records was major, and my father made sure that I understood the family's sacrifice. I was quite aware that without the yams, beans, nuts, and sweet potatoes grown on our land, we would not have been so fortunate. Even at ten years old, I knew that it would be a monumental task for me to learn English this way. In this pursuit, I listened to these records every day and through them, I gained my initial knowledge of the spoken English language. His co-workers also advised him not only to buy me a Bible so that I could practice my reading, but to try and teach me mathematics as well since he was "talented in figures" himself. My father, being the perfectionist that he was, expected me to learn how to speak and write English in record time. Therefore, he provided me with a schedule so that he could teach me mathematics as well as drawing, coloring, and the Christian religion. In today's language, I was home-schooled by my father.

Five days a week, my father would give me math homework, which he checked each night with rigor, with the exception of Saturday and Sunday. He also checked the boys' homework, and he created a reward system, giving out bonuses for work well done. For example, he gave us five candies for every fifty points for a good day's work. My father also rendered punishment for our mistakes. Punishments were sometimes actually physical. For instance, he would give out several lashes with a cane for every mistake we had made in the homework. Even today, I sometimes shiver when I remember the many times that I was whipped. This special whipping cane, which was referred to as a *Kibooko* in Luganda, was always kept under his mattress. We even tried to cut it up once with a sharp knife. When that failed, we were always hopeful that this dreaded instrument would break while in use. Sadly, I have no memory of that special cane ever breaking. In fact, it remained safely under his bed until all of us had left home. None of us kids knew how, or when, or even if that cane ever disappeared from my father's house. This system of punishments and rewards caused us to resent his returning home from work because, without fail, one of us got punished almost every day for our errors, especially in mathematics. My father would administer the lashes no matter how fatigued he was from working all day long. He had no mercy on us; he expected perfection in us.

Another punishment could be the loss of a dinner or lunch. We each prayed that such a punishment did not fall on a Friday or a Sunday. On Sundays, our dinner came with a special treat: a small but special piece of meat that my father purchased at a Western-style store from the frozen food section, and it was very expensive and tender. Oh, it was so delicious! On Fridays, we used to have smoked fish prepared in peanut sauce. For this one, you have to taste it to understand fully what I am talking about. It was something we really looked forward to eating. It was so tasty and delicious. So, whenever this type of punishment happened on a Friday or Sunday, it meant that you missed one of the best dishes of the week. And it was not easy to save it for the next day, since each individual used to have such a small serving. If you were not there, the sibling who sat next to your seat would grab it. So if you were not there, the piece of meat or fish wasn't going to be there again until the next week.

Since I didn't go to a formal school, my reward for good work also included other nice presents. For example, I use to get an extra pair of shoes, a new dress, and books, while the boys only got the candies at the end of the month. They also had only one other dressy outfit aside from their school uniforms that my father purchased. As mentioned earlier, my father was paid once a month, so presents came only once or every two months. Personally, I enjoyed each present and the special treatment; however, what I wanted most was to go to a formal school. My envy of my brothers was always multiplied when they returned to school after a school vacation. After all, they were attending the best high school in the entire country, King's College Budo.

When the boys were younger, they rode their bikes to school, but as they grew older, my father decided to buy a car to ease the costs of transportation for the family. So, around 1944, when I was about twenty, he purchased a used, old Morris automobile. It was kind of yellowish-brown with a canvas top cover, and it used to rattle loudly when driven. Yet, he was so very proud of it. After all, it was physical evidence of his personal accomplishment. He was one of the few Africans who owned a car in colonial Uganda. So, such an example of personal ownership was important to him, even though he constantly tried to tell us that the opinion of others had little impact on him. As I reflect on the past, I now think that this might have been simply another British cultural value that my father had accepted unconsciously. My father never drove his car to work, but continued to ride his bike, probably because it was cheaper, or maybe he felt that some of his European co-workers might think him to be "uppity" since he could afford to purchase a car. Regardless of the reasons, he only drove it when a number of us kids had to go someplace with him, like church on Sunday, or when we had to go somewhere but there was no public transportation. In any case, he never wanted us to go on a public bus. I remember how he enjoyed driving his personally owned car to pick up his sons from Budo. My brothers, on the other hand, were not so excited.

My brothers complained that the car made so much noise that their fellow classmates would always look in the direction of the noise to see who was coming. So, they never liked the idea of Father coming to their boarding school in his car to pick them up. They preferred instead to get a ride with the parents of a classmate. At that age, my brothers especially felt ashamed and embarrassed; not only was the car loud, but the old Morris automobile was also unsightly with its canvas hood. You see, there were some well-to-do families who visited their children in newly purchased cars like Mercedes Benzes, large, old Buicks, and Chevrolets. My brothers were on full academic scholarship. So, they and others from the same socioeconomic levels had parents who had either no car or a rattling one like my father. Even at this time, the type of car one owned could often be associated with or linked to one's economic situation. While at Budo, my brothers usually found a way to earn pocket money to meet their financial needs. In fact, they would make posters with various mottos or logos and sell them to their classmates. These posters were much desired in the old days.

My brothers would also take photographs of their fellow students for a fee, but I do not remember how and when they purchased the camera. They even sold roasted groundnuts (peanuts) at the day school they attended before entering boarding school. So, part of my brothers' success has been due to their entrepreneurial skills and their ability to be creative in their pursuits to succeed in life. I am sure that part of the hard-work ethic was transferred from our father. I do not think that my father ever questioned them about where they got this extra money, nor was he aware of their running small businesses at school. He expected them to study and to have only the school meals, period. He was not aware that the few shillings that he gave them were not enough to take them through the semester or to buy any snacks. But I must admit that our father did the best with the little he was getting as a monthly salary. Taking care of sixteen children and three adults was no joke, so he deserves credit for all of his efforts to provide us with a decent life.

Chapter 4

SYSTEMS OF EDUCATION, DOUGLAS, AND MY FATHER

In Uganda, education has never been completely compulsory. In the past, only the parents who could afford to pay sent their children to school to be formally educated. Our public and private educational systems were and are based on the British model, inclusive of curriculum. There are primary levels that go from Primary 1 to Primary 7; secondary levels—Standard 1 to Standard 4; two levels of higher secondary, or high school; then, three to five years of postsecondary education (college and/or university). Our public system requires students to take standardized exams at each level before being allowed to proceed to the next level. This intense competition for a seat in the classroom and for government scholarships continues today. When we were growing up, if a student was able to do well on the exams, he or she would be able to have his or her entire educational fees and tuition paid by the government. This was largely how my father and brothers were able to attend Budo and Makerere University. They got good grades in the elementary and secondary levels, especially in high school. This also worked to the benefit of my older brother Douglas, whom my father kicked out of the house when he was about nine or ten years old. The reasons behind my father's behavior will forever remain a mystery since both parties are long deceased.

Douglas stayed away for years; one day, I saw him on my way to the market to buy groceries. I was so surprised. He was wearing a traditional male outfit that was decorated with red and green strips around the neck. You should have seen us! We both were elated to see each other. Douglas explained to me that he was staying at the Salvation Army with many other children who didn't have homes, and that they were only allowed to wear their traditional outfit and slippers that were provided by the Salvation Army. Then he explained to me how he, along with the other boys living there, would go out in groups and tell people about God. He also told me that he had been circumcised, as if it meant something to me. Since I did not know how to act or respond I said, "Oh, ooh," with very sad emotions on my face and in my voice. As I reflect on that moment, I now know that he was happy about it. Traditionally, the Baganda did not circumcise their males. So, Douglas might have seen this as an act of rebellion. He knew that our father would have never approved of such an operation. I asked Douglas whether he would like for me to bring him anything from home, like a shirt. He replied no, explaining that the Salvation Army did not allow the children to put on any other clothing besides what the Salvation Army gave them to wear. I informed him that I would bring him his Bible. So, we planned a meeting and I took him his Bible. However, I had to sneak it out in a shopping bag while on another grocery-shopping trip.

After that meeting, I did not see him again until he was brought to my father's house by Reverend Yafesi Sempa, a friend of my father. Douglas was now in his teens. Reverend Sempa, who was the head of a boys' high school in Mengo, begged my father not only to allow Douglas to return home, but to enroll him in a reputable school. The reverend explained that he had seen Douglas with the Salvation Army group going around the Namirembe and Mengo areas spreading the Gospel. My father's response was almost unbelievable but characteristic of him. He refused to allow Douglas to return to his house, stating, "He might have picked up some bad habits while he was away that he might teach the rest of the children. Let him go somewhere else, find him a school, a boarding school, where those stupid people who kept him this long can support him." In response to my father's outburst, Reverend Yafesi said, "I can admit him into my school." And my father quickly lashed out with, "Okay, he is one hundred percent yours." Then the reverend thanked him, but also explained that Douglas would be coming home for the holidays, to which my father agreed. After two years at the Reverend's school, Douglas succeeded in earning very good grades at the lower high-school level. In fact, his grades were so good that he earned a full three-year scholarship to King's College Budo, where he was later joined by some of his other siblings. While he was enrolled at King's College Budo, Douglas never came back to the house, not even on school vacations. After graduating from King's College Budo, he was awarded a full academic scholarship to attend Makerere University. Douglas got his degree in agricultural management and worked for many years for the Ugandan Tea Estate, as well as for the Ugandan Hotels. If one tried to find Douglas in any family photos, the search would be fruitless, since he was not welcomed by my father.

My siblings knew that if they applied themselves, got good grades, and scored high on the national exams, they would not only be accepted into Makerere, but their school fees would be paid in full by the government. In fact, this was a ticket to a better life and a life outside of our father's control. However, we as a family never attended any of my brothers' high school or university graduations, because they never informed us of the dates. Moreover, when the boys left Budo and later Makerere University, they never returned home to live. In fact, they only came around when there was something that seriously required their presence.

Today in Uganda, access to a formal education is still very competitive, and competition increases as the grade level increases. So, students, especially those who grow up under very difficult circumstances or challenges, usually work very hard to pass the standard exams with high marks. They see education as an opportunity to change their destinies and the lives of their families. High scores will increase their chance for a four-year or six-year academic government scholarship. In the past, some parents were content to send their children to school just for the sake of their learning how to read and write. I believe that most parents would love to see their children accomplish more in life than themselves. A greater number of parents are also sending their children to day schools. These schools are less expensive than boarding schools and usually have less demanding admission requirements. In the last fifteen years or so, more schools, both in the private and governmental sectors, have been built. These academic institutions range from private academic institutions to technical colleges. In addition, some students will take any type of job to earn the school fees. They understand that if they are going to be useful to their community and country, they need to be educated.

There have been other additions to the Ugandan educational system. For example, the children of

Figure 3: My brother Douglas.

Figure 4: *Front row*: My sister Mary and my mother Yunia (with the scarf); *Back row*: Me behind my mother, and my brother Douglas.

parents with economic means can now start their education at an earlier age. Parents no longer have to wait to send their children to Primary 1, but can enroll them in preschool/nursery school. As in the world over, children of parents with financial means have more options. In fact, many such parents send their children to be educated out of the country, with or without high exam scores. I was very fortunate that all five of my children were accepted into very good boarding schools. We as a family were not able to pay the high-school fees without some difficulty, but we knew that we had the power within us to survive the difficulties at the moment. I know that it was only by the grace of God that my children were accepted into two of the best schools in Uganda, King's College Budo for my late son Michael and Gayaza for my four girls. I was allowed to make special payment arrangements and I felt no shame. What was important was that my children were getting a good education and that they knew that they had to work hard in order to be successful in their studies. I guess I taught them as my father taught me: Do the best in whatever you put your hands to.

Chapter 5

MY EDUCATION AND A DREAM COME TRUE

As mentioned in Chapter 3, I was eight years old when my father enrolled me in the primary school at King's College Budo. As one of the first twelve girls to be admitted, I felt more than privileged. I was ecstatic. And I was really crushed when my father took me out after only one semester. So, up until I was about fifteen, all of my schooling was more on a home-schooling basis or was self-directed. I took advantage of any and all opportunities to learn. I have often wondered why my brother Douglas and I were given such difficult paths to walk. Did we remind my father of our biological mother too much, or were we too strong in our personalities? I am so happy that neither of us allowed our somewhat negative circumstances to crush our desire to make our lives worth living.

In 1940, at the age of sixteen, I entered the Nurses' Training College (NTC) at Mengo Missionary Hospital. At first, the admissions board was very reluctant to consider my acceptance because I lacked the basic required formal education. Then, Dr. Hebe Welbourne, an English female pediatrician working in a clinic at Makerere University located near our home, intervened on my behalf. Elsie, my stepmother, who used to take us to this clinic, had apparently developed a friendly relationship with Dr. Welbourne. I am sure that one of their nonmedical discussions was about me and my desire to become a nurse in spite of my lack of formal schooling. Elsie later informed me that my father was also instrumental in my later admissions, since he had given her permission to approach Dr. Welbourne on my behalf. Dr. Welbourne agreed to speak to the appropriate persons, requesting that I be given a test to see whether I qualified for admission to the school of nursing. The exam that I took was designed to test my abilities in English—both in writing and reading—and in basic math. This meant that my scores would be the deciding factor. To their surprise, I not only passed the exam, but I passed with flying colors. In fact, I scored so high that I was given a "Special Honors Recognition Award." Furthermore, my test scores on the standard English section (both the oral and the written sections) far exceeded those of the present nursing students. On the day that I found out the news of my scores and acceptance into NTC, I was on cloud nine, as they say in the United States. Quietly to myself, I was thanking God for his goodness and mercy, my father for those English tapes and for giving me that semester at Budo, for Elsie's love and bravery in approaching Dr. Welbourne, and Dr. Welbourne for her support and intervention.

I went home that day full of excitement and positive thoughts for my future. At long last, I was in school—but not just any school. I had finally gained entrance into a bona fide school of nursing. I was elated. I now had the opportunity to learn. I told myself that I would attend each class and try very hard to grasp as much knowledge as possible. I would fill up my brain and mind so that there would be no empty spaces. Since I had passed my test with "Special Honors," I was assigned to work with the course tutor so that I could at times translate for her in some of the courses. This provided me with another opportunity to increase my knowledge and to accelerate my proficiency in the English language. My proficiency was enriched as the nursing tutor encouraged me to translate all of my class notes to English even though the other students wrote their class notes in the vernacular (Luganda). My curriculum was demanding, and the hospital assignments were rigorous. Oh, but how I enjoyed every second of it! To be honest, my stay at the school of nursing was one of the best times of my entire life. I was determined and driven to make a good life for myself.

My acceptance in nursing school also meant that I would no longer have to live at my father's house. So, after I was officially enrolled, I felt no guilt in counting the days when I would be free of my father's everyday control and rules. My nursing program provided me room and board. Therefore, I no longer had to depend on my father for anything because the colonial government of Uganda that paid for our uniforms, food, and accommodations sponsored me, like all of the other nursing students. In addition, we were given a small stipend as pocket money. There were other perks that came with my newly found independence. Since I would no longer be living with my father, my mother and my brother Douglas were now free to visit me at any time. My mother was as thrilled as I was. In fact, one of the most joyous days in my life was the first time she visited me; we talked and talked and hugged one another. She would keep marveling how nice it was that she could visit any time. She would also tell me to work hard and to be obedient to my tutors and teachers.

On some of her visits, we talked about the past and how on one of her surreptitious visits around 1933, she had given me one Ugandan shilling and told me that if I ever felt too unhappy and wanted to leave, I could use the money to take a bus and come to her place and stay with her. On that same visit, she even told me that I could teach the village children at the nearby elementary school to read and write, since I had been learning English from the tapes my father had purchased for me. At times I felt miserable, but I never dared to take off from my father's house. To leave my father's house and to travel alone with strangers on a bus was frightening to me at the time. It was even difficult for me to envision how I would get on and off a bus in a strange community located in a rural environment where I would have to look for my mother's brother's house. Even though both Elsie and my father sent me on errands to the market, I did not feel comfortable traveling alone to an unfamiliar village. So, eventually, I decided to let go, and to swallow my feelings and "just stay put." But now, in 1940, I was talking and loving my "real" mother, and we no longer had to fear being caught by my father. This, too, was a miracle.

My mother had been fortunate that the chief of Buruli had welcomed her back after my father put her out. In fact, she had been restored to her former position as the **Kabejja**, and she remained the most beloved wife of her husband until his death. And when the chief died, he left my mother and her four children some seventy acres of land to inherit. His other wives received less. My mother preserved her outward and inner beauty as she grew older. She was also very kind and was loved by many of the chief's children born to other women. As a result, she had always gotten a good share of everything, because so many children gathered at her cottage to eat and to be taken care of. In fact, many of these kids grew up thinking that they were our relatives on our mother's side. It was good for us because we knew very few of her other relatives. So, I cherished the fact that my mother and I were able really to bond with one another for the first time, but I was always saddened by the fact that I was never able to bond closely with my mother's other children, who were much older than me. The oldest died about two and a half years ago at the age of 101; however, the other three had preceded him in death.

With all of my everyday needs being taken care of by the Ugandan government, I was able to concentrate more on my studies. Subsequently, I got good grades in all of my coursework. I managed to graduate in general nursing in three years. The year was 1943; I was an eighteen-year-old African woman full of dreams and who thirsted for knowledge, but who had been denied a proper elementary and secondary education largely due to her gender and partly because she was the daughter of the traditional wife who had been sent out of the home by the husband. I used this denial to fuel my determination to succeed in life. Believe it or not, I was the first Ugandan student to do my nursing oral and written final exams in English. In this same year, I was accepted into the Midwifery Training College (MTS) at Mengo Missionary Hospital, and in 1944, at the age of nineteen, I graduated as a certified midwife, or staff nurse, a status equivalent to that of a registered nurse (RN) in the

Figure 5: My father, Festus Mawanda Kibukamusoke.

United States. In Uganda, an RN is a registered nurse with a degree in nursing and midwifery, whereas a staff nurse is registered and holds both the nursing and midwifery certificates from the Ugandan government. We did not actually have RNs at this time because the students who were enrolled for training had no opportunity to take more advanced courses; women were not yet accepted to Makerere University for degree courses. Here I was, a child who had been deliberately denied an education because of my gender. I was a girl and not worth enough for even a penny to be spent on her education. But I got it anyway, and I wore my uniform and its emblems with pride. For example, my badge had two crosses on it indicating that I was a qualified staff nurse and midwife; the blue cross signified my RN status and the red cross designated that I was a qualified midwife.

During the 1930s and 1940s, many Ugandans used to look down upon the nursing career because of some of our responsibilities involved taking care of our completely bedridden patients. So, it was considered by some to be a "dirty job" or a job for lower-class people. For some reason, we student nurses also came to the conclusion that we were forbidden to wear shoes. I do not know where we got this information. But, at the time, we actually thought only our nursing sisters from the United Kingdom were allowed to wear shoes; since our British overseers never encouraged or required us to wear shoes, we might have taken it for granted that we were not supposed to. In fact, it was not until an African girl came to work one day wearing shoes that we heard otherwise. This girl, Flora, was a daughter of a chief and, coincidentally, one of the twelve girls who had attended King's College Budo Primary School with me. One day, Flora asked me why I did not have shoes on, and she remarked that she was going to wear hers no matter what. After this conversation with Flora, I gradually started to wear mine, but only on Sundays; after all, it was my final year.

While in the medical field, I worked in several hospitals as a staff nurse, including Mengo Missionary Hospital in a senior student nurse position. In fact, I met my future husband, Yona Mukasa Mulira, while employed in this latter position. I had been assigned to work in one of the men's ward, and it happened that Yona's brother was one of my patients in the ward. Therefore, I would see Yona each time that he came to visit his brother. When we got married in 1945, my career was temporarily curtailed because my new husband did not want me to work outside of the home, and I was expected to obey his request. However, I never stopped wanting to learn more and to continue to practice my profession.

MY NURSING SCHOOL DAYS, 1940 TO 1943

Figure 6: Me with Agatha and Dorothy, friends and fellow students from Kigezi, Western Uganda; second year in nursing school, 1942.

Figure 7: Graduation from nursing school, 1943.

Chapter 6

MEETING THE MAN I MARRIED AND GROWING UP

It is now more than sixty years ago that I met the young man whom I later married. His name was Yona Mukasa Mulira, and as I mentioned earlier, when I met Yona, I was a student nurse at the missionary hospital in Mengo, located in Kampala. Yona was born on January 3, 1918, so he was about six years older than me. Whenever he came to visit his brother, he always made sure to come when I was on duty. However, I did not know this at the time. And each time he visited, he would approach me to say hello. Some days, he would even take the liberty of coming to the nurse's station to chat with us. On one of those chatty visits, he informed us at the desk that he was on leave from his military unit, which was stationed in Burma. He always looked very neat and smart in his army uniform with all of his badges clipped to his jacket, indicating his rank of sergeant in the military. He was so handsome and so nice! When he wasn't wearing his uniform, he was neatly dressed in a striped shirt and woolen gray trousers. During those days, very few men could afford to wear such attire. We girls thought highly of those few men who could afford to wear such trousers. We could even count the few families whose menfolk wore them. Such young men drove no cars, but were still highly regarded. In fact, they either walked or rode bicycles as their means of transportation. Nevertheless, the girls thought of them as special because they wore those woolen gray trousers that few families could actually afford. Fancy! I later took pride in the fact that "my man" was one of the privileged few.

Until Yona wrote me a note asking me to become his girlfriend, I had no idea that he was really interested in me. I was caught off guard. His girlfriend? Boy! At that moment, I told myself, "No, I am here to study. I am a student nurse." Therefore, my immediate reply to his request was a resounding "No!" I was a student nurse at a missionary hospital in an environment where we were being disciplined to behave, and that meant no "boyfriend business." To add fuel to the fire, I was a girl raised in my father's strict environment. So, I did not know how to handle it. I was so ignorant about having a boyfriend. I thought, also, *What will my father say if he hears I have a male friend?* All of these thoughts were racing through my mind. So, feeling awkward and stressed, I decided to avoid Yona each time he came to visit his brother. I told myself that if I ran into him, there would be no eye contact—nothing. After all, I was there to become a staff nurse. Period. To my surprise, this behavior did not deter Yona. He would say hello whether I was looking directly at him or at the wall. Usually, all he got from me in return was an occasional lousy "Hi."

Being the persistent young man that he was, Yona decided to write me a letter and to have his sister, Eseza Makumbi, give it to me. When she gave it to me, she explained how her brother wanted to establish a decent and permanent relationship with me that would lead to marriage. This man even had the guts to take a shortcut to my father. He went to my father's office and introduced himself. He told my father who he was, and that he had a sick brother at the missionary hospital where they had some very kind nurses taking care of him. He then mentioned my name among those kind nurses. Surprisingly, my father was able to put two and two together to figure out what Yona's intentions might be, because I learned that he went home that day from work in a very good mood. He told Elsie about this young man who visited him at the office and what he thought the young man was up to.

Yona's visit and my father's initial acceptance of the possibility of a marriage made for a smooth path when I later went to break the news of my pending marriage to him.

Yona officially proposed to me about three weeks before he was to return to the army. Of course, this meant that I could only have known him for six weeks at the most. After I said yes, he presented me with a beautiful Bible. This was the first and only present he gave me during the two years we were courting and engaged. We Baganda did not have the custom of giving an engagement ring, so he did not give me one. We believed in the trustworthiness of the proposal. Yona proposed; I had said yes; so there would be a wedding. The day before he was to leave, Yona came to say good-bye and to let me know that he would be gone for another two years to complete his term in the service and that he was looking forward to our marriage soon after he returned. Then, he gave me a hug and kissed me. This was my first kiss from a boy in my life. I became so nervous and immediately filled with guilt because I thought I had committed a terrible sin.

It was not easy getting that kiss from me. During those days, most girls raised in less traditional and more Westernized homes oftentimes had very little knowledge about male-female relationships prior to marriage. I grew up in an era when there was no Internet and no television with programs discussing the stages of human development. In many traditional African societies, young men and women celebrated their stages of life with a variety of initiation ceremonies. I did not participate in such rituals because my immediate family did not follow a traditional path. Also, in my own culture, it was the responsibility of a female relative of one's father (usually his oldest sister) and not the child's mother who was responsible for explaining to the growing child these changes and processes. This same relative was obligated to pass on to all of her brother's children the information about marriage and to prepare the bride-to-be for the occasion. In my case, there was no one. My father had two stepsisters, but they were never on good terms with one another. This meant that I really had no informational avenues that I could access that would have informed me about life changes, both mental and physical, as I grew up.

So, I went through my early adolescence without any real guidance or cues as to what to expect. It was scary, and I often thought that something must be wrong with me, especially when I started my menstrual cycle or when my breasts became very tender and grew. I was too nervous to discuss it with anyone for fear that I would be punished. It was not until I entered the school of nursing that I came to know what physical changes were common to all females. In addition, we seldom saw people kissing on the lips, with the exception of one English staff nurse who kissed a male friend at the hospital. We thought that it was a white person's custom. So, it was something that we culturally did not do publically. And it took me a while to get over my guilt about Yona's kiss. In the beginning, I felt so ashamed that I could not even talk to my friends about it. Therefore, I kept it to myself for months. When I finally shared it with friends, they just laughed at me. It became obvious to me that not all young African females thought that a kiss from the opposite sex was a sin.

While Yona was in the service, his brothers and sisters developed a good relationship with me. They would invite me to their homes on occasion and made sure that we became friends before Yona returned from the service. So, when I finally broke the news of the relationship and pending marriage with this handsome man I had met, and my acceptance by his family, my father was pleased. In fact, he had already made up his mind to give me the "green light" and his blessings to marry Yona. I would have had no difficulty, if asked, explaining how I had fallen in love with this man. However, I was thankful that my father did not ask for any details. Thank God! I would have been mortified.

Today many children in both traditional and nontraditional households can learn information on the stages of human development from a variety of sources, including the television, the Internet, the radio, in the home, at the theater, and while at school, especially in boarding schools that have the more recent technological devices.

At present, young people are exposed to a lot by watching television. Some of the information is negative, and some is positive, but it is still very informative about many things. In addition, the public- and private-school curriculums in Uganda today cover all that is needed for children to learn about male and female developmental stages, including human reproduction. At present, it is also common for parents, especially those with modern lifestyles, to talk to their children about life and the changes they will experience as they mature into adulthood. In addition, some parents will continue to go the traditional route, with initiation ceremonies and leaving it up to the father's oldest sister in the case of their female children. There are many other parents who would not dare let anyone but themselves explain to their children about the "birds and the bees." I know that I enjoyed doing it myself as far back as the 1960s. In fact, I found it to be very fulfilling, while my children found it to be fun. I also felt appreciated by my children, who thought me worthy to perform this function in their lives. Later on in life, when my late son Michael reached the age of thirteen in 1962, I asked one of his uncles to talk to him since his father was ill. Michael said, "Mom, you tell me whatever there is to be told and to learn. I'd rather hear it from you than another person." Such personal instruction became a family thing within our family, "the six of us," my five children and I. We developed our own way of talking about our concerns; we laughed, we joked, and we enjoyed comparing notes on whatever we learned from others. My dad had influenced me more than I knew. I, too, had instilled in my children the thirst for knowledge.

Chapter 7

DOWRY AND PRE-WEDDING TRADITIONS

I have always believed that a child belongs to both parents. But in my society, a child belonged to "the father and his clan". In fact, the child even bears a special name, chosen by the father from his own lineage. This special name denotes the father's clan so that the child's clan membership can always be traced. The only real exception to this tradition is with the Buganda royal family. Here, the child belongs to the mother's clan, but bears a royal name chosen from the list of royal names. So, in reality, the child still belongs to the father.

In the era in which I grew up, the father made all of the major decisions in the home concerning his children. At times, he might consult with select relatives on major decisions, plans, and events that directly affected his children. Whenever this happened, the birth mother had no choice but to accept whatever he and his relatives decided. In present-day Uganda, there have been some changes. For example, Ugandan parents who have more of a Western or modern lifestyle as opposed to those with a more traditional African lifestyle tend to sit with their children and discuss their future plans, including their marriage plans. What is very interesting is that many Ugandans, including in modern households, may continue to retain certain traditions in regard to marriage rituals and protocol, even though other traditions might not be continued.

In the Buganda tradition, a paternal aunt was usually invited to join in such decision-making, especially on big events like weddings. At the wedding ceremony, the father of the bride or her brother gave the bride away. Also, if for any reason the father was not able to give the wedding speech, he would usually appoint his brother or another male relative or a male friend to give the speech on his behalf. Since my father refused to give me away, my brother Roscoe did the honors. I was surprised, because he had consented to my marriage. The content of the wedding speech would always concentrate on the great qualities of the bride. But, traditionally, it was never the mother and it was always a man who spoke. I decided to break this tradition with my four female children, and I gave the speech at their wedding receptions, while my oldest daughter, Sanyu, spoke at my son Michael's wedding. At the time that my daughters married, I felt that I was the best person because I knew them from A to Z, and therefore was the best person to speak on their great day.

I have always believed that the wedding ceremony is one of those special events when a parent gets the wonderful opportunity to share with guests some of the most pleasant memories of his or her child's early years. There is no one more qualified than one's mother to share with all attendees those special moments. It provides another opportunity for the groom's family to become more acquainted with this new addition to their family. There is also a speech given on behalf of the groom by one of his family members. A wedding speech for the groom also accentuates the best qualities of the person, so that the bride and all of the guests are aware of the great person with whom she is exchanging vows. In addition, I believe that the wedding ceremony is too precious an event for another person other than a parent to share in the spotlight of the day.

In the Baganda tradition, a groom-to-be provides the parents of the bride-to-be with a "*bridal wealth*," referred to as **Omutwalo** in Luganda. It is an important customary tradition, and the tradition can be found in most African societies. The **Omutwalo, which is often referred to in Western literature as a *dowry or bridal price*,** could be anything of value, including money that the parents of the bride-to-be would expect the male who is marrying their daughter to render. The Western terms used to describe this exchange can be very misleading. Other African cultures have their own indigenous terms to denote this matrimonial transaction. In the real sense, the bride's parents do not mean to compare or equate the actual value of their daughter with the items or products requested. But it is a custom whereby the parents feel that they should not give their daughter away without some level of compensation or indemnity. After all, the parents raised her and, in some cases, educated her. The parental request is usually determined or guided by various factors, including the economic and social status of the girl's family, and therefore, can be given in goods, local currency, livestock, or in service or in kind. Today, such rituals and material requests can often vary according to the educational level of the female and the lifestyle of the girl's family as well as the ethnic group.

Among pastoral communities, there is always, even today, a number of cattle or sometimes a herd of cattle given as part of the bridal wealth transaction. At times, it might also include a live goat that came with many other gifts. It can also include a lump sum of money or a combination of the items mentioned above. In my culture, the mother of the bride would always expect an expensive traditional dress, referred to as a **Basuuti**, from the groom, and she would be expected to wear this traditional dress on her daughter's wedding day. It is this gift from the groom's family that usually came with a lump sum of money as a gift to the bride's mother. There are also similar expected gifts to be given to the father of the bride and the paternal aunt who was responsible for having tutored the bride in the ways to be a wife, as well as another special gift for the eldest brother-in-law. At most special celebrations, especially weddings, women wear a **Basuuti**, which is also referred to as a **Gomesi**. I should also mention here that the brides-to-be from other ethnic groups in Uganda do not necessarily wear the Basuuti. In fact, they might wear their own traditional dress associated with their particular cultural group, or any outfit they deem appropriate and acceptable for the occasion. Also, today, many brides will often choose a Western-style wedding dress, while the attendees might wear traditional dress styles. The Baganda groom and other important men in the wedding usually wear their traditional long white shirt that is worn over their pants, called a **Kanzu**, and the men can also wear jackets on top of the **Kanzu**. It is often mandatory that men dress up in a **Kanzu** at all major functions connected to the wedding ceremonies, but they do not necessarily have to wear it all day on the wedding day. However, there is one exception: certain males of the bridal group do have to dress in **Kanzus** all day, even on the wedding day. The **Kanzu** is considered the Baganda cultural attire for men, and it is also held up as a dignified dress style. We believe that it is indigenous to Uganda, even though some non-Baganda people have claimed that it is foreign to the area and our culture. At present, it is also not unusual for the groom and his support group to dress in Western-style suits.

So, before the actual marriage ceremony, there were usually social functions designed to better acquaint the groom-to-be's and the bride-to-be's families with one another. Among the Baganda ethnic group, such gatherings, especially if the families were well known, are still considered great social events even today. It was and is at such meetings referred to as the "Introduction," or **Kwanjula**, when the groom's relatives officially introduce themselves to the bride's relatives at her parents' home. They take numerous presents, including a cow or cows, a goat or goats, and many other goods of their choice, like **Kanzus, Gomesis**, and money, known as "the envelope," to give to the bride-to-be parents. Now, the cash is always brought in separate envelopes, hence the title "the envelope," and is given not only to the girl's parents but to that special paternal aunt as well.

Then, more envelopes with less money may also be provided to some other members of the bride-to-be's family, if the prospective groom can afford it. This is the perfect opportunity for him to ingratiate himself with his future in-laws and to make himself popular with them. The more envelopes he brings, the better, because it is interpreted as a sign that the groom, his family, and his friends are prepared not only to be friendly, but are also financially able to provide a good life for the bride-to-be. This is extremely important since marriage, traditionally, has been seen as a bond of families and not an individual act or just a decision between the bride and the groom. At this time, the groom-to-be and his parents would also mention the date they intend the marriage to take place.

As part of the bride price, parents also tried to make sure that they requested something that would last for a period of time that would remind them of their daughter. This was a way of keeping the daughter close even after she had married and moved in with her husband. Parents also believed that asking for a large gift would indicate that their daughter was considered valuable and precious. Furthermore, it let the groom-to-be know that it would not be easy for him simply to come and take their child without some type of indemnity. So, the *bridal wealth* was extremely important in the relationship of the two families that were being joined. In some cultures, when the groom-to-be went to ask for the hand of the young lady, he generally took some members of his age group (friends and relatives) to assist in negotiating the *bridal price* or compensation. This action could also take place at a larger gathering.

I remember one such social gathering many years ago where two to four large containers of customary beer were brought in that had been specially brewed for the happy occasion. The attendees arrived with different kinds of gifts, no matter the cost. So, the goods were put down, and then the chairman, usually the brother of the girl, requested a glass of the traditional beer to taste. He had to make sure that it was properly concentrated and tasted good. After he announced that it was good and delicious, the attendees joyfully clapped their hands. Then and only then could the drinking begin for both bridal and groom party groups. It is also the chairman who gives the green light for the marriage plans to go ahead. When the **bridal wealth** negotiations and wedding discussions took place over drinking, it could take two to three hours, or longer, to reach a consensus. The chairman would try to complicate the negotiations so as to make it appear difficult. But it was all mock seriousness that ended gleefully.

My father never requested a bridal price for me. He said that it was like bargaining your own child for a price. He used to say that he would "never find any price suitable—his children were not for sale," but that "no one could afford the price if his children were for sale." Of course, this was a very Westernized view of the bride-price tradition, but it also illustrated the independent nature of my father. Today, there are many Ugandans who decide not to ask for an **Omutwalo**; for those who do, they are usually more expensive than in the past. For some, it is more of who can outdo or overshadow the other. Even though I did not receive a dowry for my four daughters, I wanted the men who married them to know that my children were and would always be my precious children, and that once they married my daughters, they became my precious sons. Fortunately, I was blessed that all of my son-in-laws and my daughter-in-law turned out to be wonderful and loving people. I love them dearly, especially since they are now the loving parents of my lovely grandchildren. I am so thankful to God for such blessings.

TRADITIONAL DRESS STYLES: THE BASUUTI AND THE KANZU

Figure 8: Young men wearing the traditional Kanzu with my son Michael second from the left.

Figure 9: At the wedding of Sala Mirembe with the bride wearing a Western-style dress, groom wearing a Kanzu, and several guests wearing a Basuuti.

Chapter 8

MARRIAGE PREPARATION AND MY "LADY OF HONOR"

I got married on December 1, 1945, at the age of twenty-one. Rebecca Mulira (a very close friend and also my sister-in-law) and I made my wedding dress because it was impossible to find a ready-made one in the stores that I could afford. This was during World War II, and the stores not only lacked sufficient merchandise, but the available merchandise was extremely overpriced. And this was especially true for imported items. So, I designed my wedding gown using fine velvet material, while Rebecca, wife of my husband's eldest brother, designed the veil for me. She used a piece of mosquito netting long enough to make the trail. I did the embroidery on the veil, and Rebecca designed the headpiece with some fresh flowers that were able to last for at least two days. I do not remember the name of the flowers, but they were beautiful to the eyes and sweet to smell. In the end, both the homemade gown and veil were not only gorgeous, but, they fitted the purpose beautifully. My fiancé bought me a pair of shoes, and I also took a second pair of shoes to change into. I did not care that I only had two pairs of shoes to my name, nor was I saddened by my lack of expensive material possessions for my wedding. On my wedding day, I was beside myself. I was going to marry one of the most desirable bachelors in Kampala. In addition, I would never have to adhere to any of my father's rules again.

The first person I asked to be my matron of honor or "lady of honor" refused me. She was a friend of my stepmother Elsie, and I will refer to her as Mrs. B. I was so shocked when her immediate response was "No." She was one of the few ladies of the time whom I saw as being dignified, and I admired her. Mrs. B. was not only from a prestigious and high-profile family, but she was married to a very wealthy man from the very prominent Kisosonkole family. So, both Mrs. B. and her husband moved with the people in high circles, so to speak. At the time that I asked her, I was not thinking of our socioeconomic class difference. I just admired her and I wanted her to grace me with her presence on one of the greatest days of my life. When she refused, I was at a loss as to whom to approach next, because her refusal had made me lose some of my self-confidence. I was young and had been raised in a very sheltered family atmosphere. So, I did not know many people, and I really had no idea of where to go and find the person to serve as my "lady of honor." Furthermore, I had no knowledge that the "lady of honor" should be a close friend or a female relative. But, when I told Rebecca of Mrs. B.'s refusal, Rebecca quickly offered to serve as my "lady of honor," saying, "Oh, Faith we love you and we would like you to join our family. Yes, I will be your lady of honor." In fact, Rebecca and I had become true friends even before Yona's return from military service. She was such a wonderful lady, and I continue to cherish the deep friendship that developed between us. She reminisced about the joyous event of that day when I joined the Mulira family for years. Unfortunately, she died in a car accident about five years ago.

As I reflect, it is obvious that I was very naïve about marriage and life in general. I thought that marriage would automatically make me not only a person with dignity, but a respectable married woman as well. At the time, I did not fully recognize that I was already a person with dignity. Being inexperienced about real life, I was looking forward to wearing a wedding ring on my finger and becoming a wife and a mother. Interestingly enough, my fiancé remembered only a day before our wedding day that we needed rings to take with us to the church. During those World War II days, there were no jewelry shops in Kampala with reasonable prices, so he went and bought inexpensive finger bands from a nearby Ugandan bookstore for one Ugandan shilling, which was equivalent to fifty U.S. cents at the time. Traditionally, engagement rings and wedding rings were not part of our wedding ceremonies, but by this time, we had accepted this Western exchanging-of-wedding-rings tradition.

So, I openly admit that I had many hazy ideas as to what marriage entailed. In reality, I had never thought about the commitment that went with it. I had always admired and envisioned successful and happily married women as those who were nicely dressed in silky, long-sleeved dresses brought from London. I wanted very much to be associated with those women who wore large, wide-brimmed hats, held long umbrellas as a walking stick, and were having children. This was the image of marriage that I had in my mind, and it was epitomized and represented by Mrs. B. At the time, it never occurred to me that those fantasized images were connected with having a certain financial status that allowed one the freedom to purchase whatever one desired, like silky, long-sleeved dresses. Today, in Uganda, I do not see women wearing such things that attract me to that degree.

Chapter 9

THE WEDDING, THE AFTER-PARTY, AND THE HONEYMOON

My wedding day had been set for Saturday, December 1, 1945, which was two months after Yona's return from military service. At this time, Yona was living not at his father's house but at his older brother's house. All of the arrangements had been made, and I had waited two long years to be joined in matrimony with my husband-to-be. The wedding ceremony was to be held at St. Paul's Cathedral in Kampala. This was the most prestigious place at the time to get married. I was so excited. During those days, it was against our custom for a girl to go visit or go out alone with the boyfriend whom she intended to marry. So, there was very little time for both parties to really get to know each other. I did enjoy the fact that for about a month before the actual exchange of vows, the bride-to-be gets VIP care at her parents' home. She is highly pampered there and is required by tradition to reside in the house most of the time until the wedding. She is assisted in showering, and the individual chosen to take care of her helps to rub oil or cream all over her body every day. The future bride is not allowed to do any house chores. She is simply supposed to relax and rest as much as she can before her busy life as a wife and mother begins.

These restrictive rules and this pampering treatment apply only to the bride-to-be. Such special treatment makes the future bride feel so special and leaves her thinking that she will also be similarly treated once married. The night before the wedding day, there is always an **Akasiki** celebration. This is a party held at both places—one at the girl's home and one at the boy's home. People dance, rejoice, and feast on a whole roasted goat or pig and chicken cooked over an outside fire and well-wishing people would surround the fire the entire night. The **Akasiki** on the groom's side is referred to in English as the "bachelor's party." It is still common for many of the guests to go to the wedding, the wedding reception, and the after-party with a hangover from the **Akasiki**. Our **Akasiki** took place on Friday, November 30, 1945. And we left early, because my fiancé and I had to go to the church early in the morning hours for counseling and to take Holy Communion, as was the tradition of our church. Our wedding was scheduled for 3:00 P.M. on that Saturday afternoon, so, after the church, Yona took me back to my father's house, and then he returned to his older brother's house, anxiously awaiting the wedding ceremony.

When I arrived back at my father's house, I found that a large number of guests had arrived and were already enjoying themselves with the drinks they had brought with them. I was also hit with some news that not only tore me asunder but almost led to the cancelation of the wedding service. My stepmother Elsie informed me that my mother would not be allowed to attend the celebration because my father had sent her away while I was at the church. I was beside myself. I can still remember the incident and the sequence of questions that left me stunned:

> "My mother will not come to my wedding?" I asked.
> "No, she was sent away," Elsie replied.
> "Why?" [a moment of silence]
> "But, why?" I asked again, so perplexed.
> "Well, she is not going to come," she said. "Your father sent her away when she came this morning."
> "What happened? What was the reason?" I asked.

"Your father said that because she was never here when you were growing up, therefore, she should not participate in your wedding celebration."

"My mother will not come to my wedding?" I asked again. I was beginning to feel so angry.

"Then who is coming if my mother is not coming?" I asked.

"Your father will not let her come," my stepmother answered hastily.

"*Then there will be no wedding!*" I said angrily.

Then, I walked out through the door and walked away.

"*No wedding,*" I emphasized. "*There will be no need for a wedding.*"

As a bride-to-be, I was not supposed to walk on the public street, especially not alone. I was expected to be calm and remain homebound until the time of the ceremony. I, a child who was supposed to be seen and not heard, had to walk out of her father's house on her long-awaited wedding day to make a point. By doing so, I had defied tradition, and I did not even know where I was going. People could not believe what they were witnessing, so they started to panic and tried to stop me. They shouted, "Hey! Do not go!" "You cannot do that, come back." "Are you crazy?" they yelled at me. "You cannot do this to us." "Come back. Do not go. Come back." "Where is she going? She is crazy." They were beside themselves.

I continued to walk away. I did not pay attention to them. A child is to be seen, not heard, but I was going away from the house in view of everyone. Some of the guests followed me, shouting, "What's wrong with you? Boy! We can't believe this! Come back. Girl, are you crazy?" Eventually, a man came running to tell me that my mother not only would be attending the wedding celebration at the church, but would come to the house as well, so I should go back to my father's house. I was hurting for myself and for my mother as tears ran down my cheeks. When I returned, my father did not say a word to me, nor did he ever offer an apology. I had offended and embarrassed him with my actions, but I had to take a stand. This was supposed to be my great day. I could tell that some of my relatives did not support what my father had done even though they did not confront him. But I heard some of them saying, "Well, the girl should know that her father can very easily do such a thing, because Festo very Baada—Festo the bad guy—would do anything. That's just him, Festo will never change." Well, I had decided I could not take it anymore. It was my day, and on my great day I was not going to stand for any nonsense from my father. That is why I walked away: to show my frustration.

By the time I returned to the house, my mother had already gone to the church and was waiting for the ceremony to start. The wedding vows went off beautifully and without incident. It was normal to take a photograph of the wedding party outside of the church immediately following the ceremony, since the church minister might not be able to attend the reception. When I looked around, I did not see my mother. I was again infuriated when I realized that my mother had not been given a seat with the wedding party to take the photograph. When I finally located her far in the back standing among the crowd, I immediately requested that she be brought closer to me. She was then positioned to stand right behind me, over my left shoulder.

In Africa and especially in Uganda, weddings are usually big family events, with few exceptions. The extended families and friends on both sides attend whether they are invited or not. At present, the younger generations oftentimes send out invitations to limit the attendance and to get a better count for catering. At my wedding, there were at least two hundred seventy-five persons. Only half of the attendees were able to attend the reception. And not every guest was able to attend the church service due to the lack of adequate transportation. So, half of the guest waited at home dancing and sipping on the beers they brought with them. Everything was so expensive, to the extent that we could only afford to serve roasted nuts and bread-and-butter sandwiches with a cup of tea. My father refused to buy any alcoholic drinks, but he did buy soft drinks. I am not sure whether this was for economic reasons or religious convictions. Nevertheless, I was very happy to see that some guests had brought their own beers. Of course, many of my guests had already enjoyed the roasted goat at the **Akasiki** the night before. We just could not afford expensive edibles in the era of World War II. But it was still the big wedding of the season at the most prestigious church in Kampala.

As I mentioned previously, transportation was an issue for many of my guests. My father, to my surprise, got a big kick out of having to transport people in his personal automobile from the church to the reception at his house. He had to make several trips in the old Morris car. It was my good fortune that he did not mind doing it. In fact, his willingness and joyfulness to do this turned the atmosphere of the day into more of a gala celebration. He seemed to have gotten pleasure knowing he was one of the few who had a working automobile. My mother ended up not only attending both the church service and the reception, but rode in my father's car from the church to the house. What a great day! My father had redeemed himself, and I felt so good and so special. What made the day even more special was the fact that I was the first child of my father to get married. In the end, everything went smoothly, and Yona and I left for our honeymoon after the reception and the after-party.

I must admit, there were times when I thought that the reception and later the after-party would never end. But as soon as they did end, I realized that I would have to leave my mother and other relatives behind. It was at that point that I began to feel sad, especially after my mother explained that she had developed a fever while we were saying our good-byes. So, I left for my honeymoon with reluctance. We had to travel more than fifty miles to get to our honeymoon destination. Some members of my husband's wedding party accompanied us, and they were rejoicing and singing all the way. I was so nervous, and my mind was clouded with a lot of uncertainty. After some two hours, we arrived at our destination in a town called Jinja in Busoga country, some fifty miles from Kampala.

Figure 10: St. Paul's Cathedral, where my wedding took place, located on Namirembe Hill.

Figure 11: My wedding, December 1, 1945, at St. Paul's Cathedral.

Our honeymoon was more like a kind of one-day party even though we spent two whole days there. By the time we reached the house where we would be staying, it was around 8:00 P.M. and already dark outside. I was so tired after a long wedding day and so uncertain as to what was coming ahead of us in regard to the after-wedding celebrations.

Upon our arrival, we found crowds of people singing, dancing, jumping, and beating drums. All of them were dressed up in fancy dresses to make the ceremony special for the brother of their **Gombolola** chief/district sub-county chief (and a representative of the Kabaka's government), whose name was Assy. So, all of this meant a lot to the entire community. The actual festivities were held at his house located only eight miles from Jinja at Ntenjeru. As you may recall from the introduction of this book, Jinja is where the Nile River starts. Some people joined the festivities simply to please the chief, while others joined just to have fun or both. We did not have dinner until about 10:30 P.M., and we were not expected to leave the party until 12:00 A.M. However, we found a way to escape quietly from the party, which continued until dawn. You would never have known that there was a worldwide depression, because there was plenty of everything—food, drinks, singing, dancing, and fun-filled noise. It was too much for me, having been raised up in an isolated home environment. And, when I immediately realized that I had no idea of what I had gotten into or what marriage was all about, I became very homesick. But, with the great treatment from our hosts, my new husband and I happily survived the two days of our honeymoon. Assy had only one wife at that time. I guess he had to set a good example for his younger brother Yona. We were given two goats, trays of eggs, **matooke** (green plantain bananas that would later be mashed and steamed in a pot, usually over a charcoal stove covered with banana leaves), and six live chickens to take back with us to Kampala. I was impressed with how my husband's relatives treated me like a queen. Still, I was overwhelmed with everything. I had grown up in an overprotected home environment, and I had no realistic ideas of what came after the wedding ceremony.

Figure 12: Wedding party and guests in front of St. Paul's Cathedral; my mother is directly over my left shoulder.

Chapter 10

MY MARRIAGE YEARS

Even though I was twenty-one years old, I was an innocent child who understood neither the real responsibilities of a marriage nor money matters. Before getting married, money was not something that I had to dwell on. My nursing program had provided for everything, and prior to that, my father had. Sometimes, I wish for a return of those days of innocence. But as you know, sometimes innocence is no more than naivety or immaturity after a certain age. I actually went into my marriage without any concern as to whether the man I was marrying had an income for us to live on. At the time, I honestly never thought about it. But as I reflect, I think that at a subconscious level, I had assumed, like the public, that my groom had sufficient monies. After all, Yona was from a well-placed family. In fact, he was royalty from the Kingdom of Kooki, an ancient traditional chiefdom in the Rakai District of South Central Uganda that was incorporated into the Buganda Kingdom sometime in the 1890s. However, its royal line has continued to the present and is currently led by Kamuswaga Apollo Sansa Kabumbuli II. So, my Yona was a prince from Kooki. In addition, his brother Assy was an official representative of the Kabaka's Government. Furthermore, Yona was an ex-serviceman, and there was a general belief that all former service personnel had tons of money. But, at the same time, I did not realize that there was no money for them to have, especially since their term of service was over.

During the two years of our engagement, we never discussed how Yona would support the family. I just wanted to be married so that our perfect life could get started. However, I do vaguely remember that very close to the marriage ceremony, Yona mentioned that he was looking for a job, but I was not disturbed by his news. Well, once the ceremony and festivities were over, I was quickly awakened to the harsh realities of our financial situation. Within two weeks of our marriage, we found ourselves with no money. Yona had spent whatever money he brought into the marriage, and I found out that my newly wedded spouse had no means to support us. I discovered that I had married a man who had no money, no job, and no bank account. By profession, he was a surveyor, but during a global economic depression, the jobs were few and far between. It took him a good six months to secure a job as a government surveyor. In the end, he also decided to return to school part-time to train as a civil engineer. His pride as a young Muganda man, and as a young ex-serviceman, led to his wanting to be the sole provider for our family. So, he did not want me to go back to work, and I was expected to acquiesce to his dream. So, I left my job. This created some level of marital discord and economic pressure in our household. Fortunately for us, one of our most cherished cultural traditions assisted in our survival, especially the first few years of our marriage. Friends and neighbors would usually bring plenty of presents, fruits, and other foods (including chickens and eggs) to newly wedded residents in their community as a way to wish them good luck and to be fruitful and to multiply. Sometimes, they even brought a live goat to slaughter and to roast over an outdoor fire. At such times, the new couple, along with the guests, would feast together. I have been told that such traditions are no longer the norm in Uganda, and that individuals are now more concerned with their own individual survival. This is understandable given the trials and hardship all Ugandans have had to face due to prior civil wars and economic crises.

In 1948, we were blessed with our first child, a little girl whom we named Sanyu, which means "peace and joy." We later had four more children: Michael was born in 1949, Mabel in 1951, Irene in 1953, and Damali in 1955. I loved my husband and adored my children, but I found that I was depressed a lot. Initially, my husband, who was older and more mature than I, had great patience. He really did love me from the beginning and was happy about our family. He also tried to nurture me as I went through various stages of transitioning into my married life and my role as a mother. Yona was a nice, handsome man and loving person who had everything going for him but one thing. He was sick with the disease of alcoholism. I did not know this before we married, and he was very careful to hide it. But as the disease progressed, there came a time when he could no longer hide it from me. We dragged on with the marriage until it reached an unbearable stage for the kids and me. So, the first ten years of the marriage was full of ups and downs, and I was emotionally and verbally abused when he was drunk. Things got progressively worse as Yona's inability to support the family became obvious. In an attempt to start over, we as a family moved to Tanzania during the years 1952 to 1955 with Yona. He had been offered a job by the Tanzanian government as an engineer to build and to supervise the construction of the government houses in the Bukoba District. Then, later, he was transferred to work in the Karagwe District. While there, I was temporarily hired as a midwife at a nearby hospital in Karagwe, even though Yona was not that thrilled about my working. This was not an unpleasant experience for us as a family because we were all together. The children were too young for school, with the exception of Sanyu, my eldest daughter, who had started going to school in Kampala. I did not enroll Michael and Mabel in school until we returned to Uganda in 1955, because they were not school-aged. And, my last two children, Irene and Damali, were actually born while we were in Tanzania. However, I gave birth to them in Uganda, where there were better-equipped maternity services and where I knew people in the medical field.

Once we returned to Uganda in 1955, we moved into a house on the property that Yona had inherited from his father. Unfortunately, Yona resumed his old habits soon after we settled in. I tried and tried to make the marriage work, and I was determined not to go back to my father's house. However, I could not make it work, and more important, I did not want my children to grow up watching their father drink himself to death. There were no Alcoholics Anonymous (AA) meetings or similar secular or nonsecular programs at my disposal. In fact, in Uganda, it was not seen as a disease. So, alcoholics either drank themselves to death or found the strength to stop through what might be referred to as self-help connections. When my oldest daughter finished high school and went to the United States, she learned about the AA program. She wanted very much to bring her father to the United States to be treated, but we lacked the funds to enable her to bring him over.

It wasn't long before Yona was unable to keep any of the jobs he acquired. Still, he did not want to let me go back to work full-time. After we returned to Uganda, he would sometimes sell a piece of the land we had whenever we needed money and whenever he needed money for drinking. Realizing that the situation was getting extremely volatile and desperate, I made plans to leave and to get a job as well as a legal separation. I thought that that would force Yona to come to his senses and realize that at least one of us needed to have stable and continuous employment.

One day in 1956 after my husband had left the house to go drinking with his elder brother, who was visiting, I put my plan in motion. I got up early the following morning and, when I saw that Yona and his brother had not returned, packed a few of my belongings. I also got my children up; we got on a bus and we took off to my mother's house. Sanyu, my oldest daughter, was at Gayaza Boarding School some twelve miles from Kampala, which went from the primary levels through the twelfth grade. But I took the other children and left them with my mother at her home. I also left a note for Yona, explaining briefly why I had left with the children.

In my note to my husband, I informed him that I had to obtain a job and be able to work for the sake of our growing children, but I did not disclose where I would be. Later, I was informed that my husband was in a state of shock after reading my note, because he never believed such a thing could happen. I knew that the first place he would think of looking for us was at my mother's place. And he did just that. He arrived there late one night, very drunk. He was so drunk that he passed out and did not wake up until late the next morning. Yona was so embarrassed that he could not bring himself to face my mother. So he left and returned some two days later to get the children after he had sobered up.

By the time that Yona woke up on that fateful day, I had already gone to catch a boat at Port Bell heading for Kisumu in Kenya, where I had already secured a one-year job assignment at a hospital in Migori, some forty miles from Kisumu, which was about eighty miles from the capital city of Nairobi. I was later told that Yona had gone two days without drinking when trying to locate me. That must have been during the time that he went to pick up the children. I had made sure to leave contact information with some trustworthy people at home so that they could let me know how the kids were doing. It was a very painful burden to shoulder, leaving my children behind and not knowing what might come of them. I had to swallow such thoughts because I had to try and make life better for them. I kept hoping that when I returned, Yona would allow me to work.

That night en route to Kisumu, I stopped at the hospital where my brother Shemmie was lying sick to ask him to let me have a few shillings to buy a Primus stove and an iron. But I lost both of them to theft on the bus route to Kisumu and Migori, where I was stationed to work. Unfortunately, without the stove and the iron, I was not able to make my own meals or to iron my clothes. So, when I got to Migori, I had to wait until I got my first paycheck before I could make my own meals. Meanwhile, my fellow nurses offered to share their meals and an iron with me. The food choices were different from what I was used to. For example, their meals included **ugali** (a mesh made with maize flour into a kind of dough) and not **matooke** as a staple. They ate it with meat, fish, or chicken and vegetables. We had very good meals, but I was not familiar with cooking the chicken whole—that is, cooking it with its legs, toes, and beak intact. On my first plate, I was served a chicken leg (not thigh) and toes with other pieces of meat. The next day, the beak was on my plate. Gosh! What an experience! I was instructed to suck the juice (soup) from the beak. "It tastes good," they said. I found it difficult to eat, but I couldn't refuse no matter how unappetizing it looked to me. I was hungry, so I ate the ugali and the soup, but not the feet, the toes, and the beak. I had to draw a line. *My God*, I said, *this is it!* My friends were so surprised that we in Uganda did not eat such chicken parts. So, they used to pick them from my plate and eat them joyfully.

Within nine months, my whereabouts had leaked out to my husband. So, he set out to find me in Migori, which was situated far away in a remote area populated largely by the Maasai people. This particular ethnic group is still known for their bravery and refusal to be Westernized. I remember one day I saw a group of Maasai running toward me in a somewhat frantic manner; some had their spears. I became very concerned with them approaching me in such a manner, so I became nervous. Once they got closer, I noticed that they were actually carrying a female who was in labor and that there was nothing to fear. At present, most of the members of this ethnic group in Kenya continue to live a very traditional lifestyle. And therefore, they constitute Kenya's main nomadic cattle group that lures many tourists to Kenya each year. They decorate their faces with different colors and usually wear no smiles. They are pastoralists and believe that all cattle were given to them at the world's creation. Therefore, the raiding of others for cattle is not considered a crime to them. They even decorate their cattle and provide them with names. Today, the Maasai continue to practice both female and male circumcision. They also continue the practice whereby they pull their ear lobes to make large elongated holes so as to wear big, rounded, and sometime very long earrings. So, when Yona arrived and witnessed both men and women carrying around spears on a daily basis, he got nervous and asked me why I had moved so far away. Since he was finally listening to me, I explained to him that I had always wanted to work to help support our children, but that he wouldn't let me. Yet he was without steady employment. He then wrote a letter while there giving me permission to work, and requested that I return to Uganda.

When I returned from Kenya in 1957, I brought his letter back with me and submitted it to the medical headquarters in Uganda. Yona promised me that he would never again interfere with my employment, and that I could work until such time that we got back together. However, he was quite adamant about not releasing the children to me immediately. According to him and our culture, the children belong to a man. I thought to myself, "to a man, indeed!" Deep down in my soul, I knew that he was going to let them come to me sooner or later. After some six to seven months, he surrendered the children to me, saying that he wasn't able to cope with them without me. He left, saying that I should do my share until I got tired, and at that point I should return them to him. That was in 1957, and until now, I have never gotten tired of my children.

My children had experienced difficult times without me, and there were days when their father was nowhere to be found. After I returned to Kampala, I would visit my children at their father's house, but it was always extremely difficult when I had to leave after visiting them. It always hurt so much to leave them behind. Even today, whenever they discuss this time of our lives, the heartbroken tone continues. They say that every time the train passed their father's house when I was in Kenya, they would go outside expecting me to be on it. So, with such expectation, they used to sing continuously, "Maama ajja, Maama ajja," meaning, "Mom is coming." No matter how many times a day the train passed their house, they repeated the same words, but Maama did not show up!

So, in 1957 when I returned to Uganda from Kenya, I was able to go back to work full-time. I had a night shift and worked from 4:30 P.M. to 6:00 A.M., and after a few months, I also had my children back with me. I left Sanyu, my eldest, who was almost nine years old, to take care of her siblings whenever she was home from boarding school. She would give them their evening meals, put them to bed, and then lock the doors. We all shared one room at the nurse's hostel, all six of us. We managed to live on my very meager income, but I had no funds to hire anyone to help me, nor could I afford to rent a better place. But we survived. Family members on both sides were not really that supportive of my decision to leave my husband and to shoulder the responsibility of parenting my children single-handed. I was thirty-two years old and I was determined to do it, and to do it with the help of the Lord in addition to my friends, including my church friends.

A year later, in 1958, I was able to purchase a moped (a bicycle propelled by a small motor) for our transportation purposes. I paid 400 shillings for it when I was working as a staff nurse on a monthly wage of 240 Ugandan shil-

Figure 13: The six of us in Tanzania, 1954.

lings. I kept this valuable asset for some two years. I used it for shopping and for transporting my children back and forth to their boarding schools. The younger ones usually walked to school because they were in close proximity. But sometimes I had to take the others to school one by one on the back of my scooter motorcycle. My society did not approve of women riding mopeds, but I had no choice but to break with cultural norms. I rode the moped all the time, and people used to stop and stare at me. Many saw me as a woman acting like I was a man. They were so amazed to see me rushing down the road. I must admit I rode that moped proudly and fiercely. Sometimes, the stares would cause me to reflect back to the times when my father sent me on errands on the bicycle and how people stared so hard in disapproval that I would stop pedaling when I saw someone I knew coming toward me. Riding bicycles, too, was seen as a male's prerogative. I think that I might have been the first woman to ride a moped on the streets of Kampala, Uganda. My children and I didn't live our lives based on others. It didn't really matter what people said; we were about surviving in a way that God would be proud of us. It still amazes me today of how many of my father's values I had made my own.

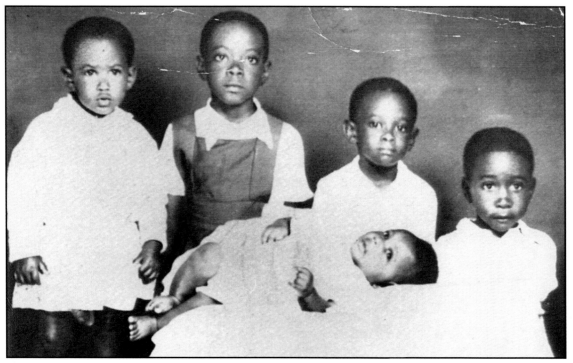
Figure 14: The five children in Tanzania, 1955.

Chapter 11

MY INITIAL EMPLOYMENT AT SANYU BABIES HOME

Sanyu Babies Home (SBH), the oldest orphanage in Uganda, is a nonprofit home for orphan children. It is situated on Namirembe Hill just below St. Paul's Cathedral, where I got married. This is a great location because it overlooks Kampala City. It was established in 1929 as a venture of faith, love, and hope by a missionary sister, the late Ms. Milnes Winfred Walker, who wanted to receive and care for abandoned, destitute, and parentless children. At the time of its establishment, Ms. Walker was the sister in charge of the maternity home and of the midwives' training school at the Church of Uganda Hospital (now the Mengo Missionary Hospital), where a number of babies were being abandoned by their birth mothers. Initially, she would take these babies one by one and care for them at her home. As their numbers grew, this was no longer feasible. So, she was able to obtain some land and a cottage from the Church of Uganda, with which she officially started SBH.

Ms. Walker was especially concerned about a local traditional belief system among some of the citizens of Uganda that led to an increase in abandoned babies. That belief system contended that babies whose mothers had died in childbirth were not only considered cursed but also viewed as having killed their mothers. Such infants were usually disowned and abandoned by their relatives. Ms. Walker and her mission supporters desperately wanted to change the fate of these abandoned and rejected children. To do this, they knew that they would also have to find a way to change the fundamental attitudes of those Ugandans who held such traditional beliefs about the children whose mothers died in childbirth. So, Ms, Walker and her supporters set out to convince these traditional believers that these precious infants were innocent victims of a terrible tragedy, not criminals, and therefore, had the right to be loved and to live full lives.

So, the initial SBH was situated near what is now Mengo Missionary Hospital, where I did my nursing training and met my husband Yona. In fact, we use to be sent to work at this orphanage almost as a punishment, and there could be fifteen to eighteen babies there at any given time. As the numbers of infants increased, the governing board of the home decided to recruit someone with nursing skills as a full-time employer who would help to implement the board's policies and to enforce its rules. Its members believed that such policies and rules would have a positive impact on the children at SBH. After learning of this full-time position, I decided to apply. I had the medical background as well as the work experience. I had worked as a staff nurse in various hospitals in Uganda, in Tanzania, and in Kenya, and I had very strong recommendations from my previous supervisors, in addition to one from Dr. Hebe Welbourne. An English lady from England was recruited and appointed as the administrator, and I was hired as her assistant with the title of Deputy Administrator. So, in 1958, I immediately resigned from my staff-nurse position at the Hospital and accepted this new employment, which came with housing and other job-related benefits.

I was so excited, and my new job was amazing. Here, I was expected to make a difference in the lives of these unwanted children at the very orphanage where I was once sent to work as a punishment. Even more amazing was the fact that I, whose relatives had tried to convince my father that I did not need a formal education, had been hired as the Deputy Administrator of Uganda's first orphanage. This was indeed a very prestigious and high-profile position for an African female during Uganda's colonial period. I can only think what must have gone through the minds of those relatives who never wished me well.

During the very next year, a new building for the babies, a cottage house, and a building for the student nursery nurses were constructed under the umbrella of the Church of Uganda. The cottage house was able to accommodate some forty to fifty babies at one time. Later on, the entire environment was further changed when other buildings were built for the staff and student assistants in 1960 and 1961. Then, in 1965, a guest house was built by the Rotary Club Association, and later, in 1975, an office facility was constructed in memory of the pioneer orphan of SBH, the Reverend Canon Benon Lwanga. Reverend Lwanga became a very prominent member of the clergy at the Namirembe Cathedral (St. Paul's Cathedral), and he also served on the SBH board of directors as the chairman for many years.

It was great to see our facilities grow. We never turned any babies away, so work at SBH was always demanding but extremely satisfying and rewarding. My presence at SBH was no longer a punishment assignment; I saw it as a blessed responsibility. I also organized the legal placement of children through adoption or by finding foster parents in the local community. I must admit, it was sometimes difficult to find local qualifying persons who would wholeheartedly commit to caring for these babies, especially those innocent victims of local traditional societal beliefs. Many people continued to hold onto traditional beliefs about these orphans. In an attempt to respond to this need, the governing board as early as 1957 had established with the help of SBH's proud pioneer offspring, the Reverend Lwanga, a two-year training program for the nursery's nursing workers. The training program was very successful and was recognized by the National Nurses Examination Board in the United Kingdom under the umbrella of Dr. Barnadoe's Homes. We used to accommodate as many as twenty-four students at any one time.

During the two years, each student was expected to be personally responsible for at least one child under the age of one year. In addition, they were expected to create a motherly childcare relationship with the child they chose or were assigned. Therefore, they were required to make outfits for the baby, even to knit a sweater for the child as well as to make him or her a toy. The student's performance would be evaluated at the end of the two years to determine whether he or she had successfully completed the program. As a result of the program's overwhelming success, SBH became a role model for any proposed childcare-agency program in Uganda. Eventually, the returning of the orphan babies to their local communities became the responsibility of a newly created government department, the Department of Social Work and Community Development. In the pursuit of strengthening this new department, the Ugandan colonial government awarded me a scholarship in 1959 to go abroad to the United Kingdom for further studies. However, it was my responsibility to not only apply to an appropriate academic institution for admission, but to get accepted. There were a total of seven Ugandans who were awarded scholarships to go abroad for further study. And once we arrived in Europe, we were joined by several others persons from different countries.

Figure 15: We six at SBH.

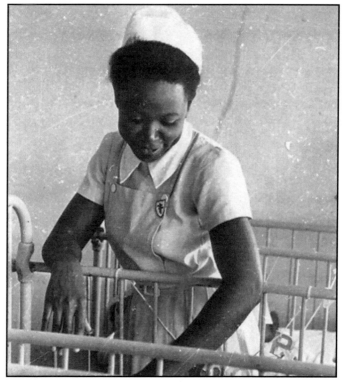

Figure 16a: Me as Deputy Administrator of SBH.

Figure 16b: SBH students playing with children in the garden at SBH.

Figure 16c: Easter party for SBH children at SBH.

Figure 16d: Children at SBH in the garden waiting to be fostered.

Figure 16e: Children of SBH at a party at a friend's house.

Figure 16f: Staff Housing at SBH.

Chapter 12

MY UK EXPERIENCE

So, eventually, I was admitted to the South Wales University College of Swansea in the United Kingdom for a two-year program in social work, concentrating on social administration, social-work services, childcare casework, and related services. We, as a group, were all assigned to study social work and community development, but I personally majored in or emphasized childcare. This two-year experience (1962–64) provided me with opportunities to work with different international organizations whose emphasis or field of study was on childcare in the United Kingdom. So, I worked with disturbed children of all ages, handicapped children, and adoption and foster-care families. For example, in the United Kingdom, we visited Dr. Barnardoe's Homes for Children and were assigned to work in the homes for two months. These homes not only received babies for adoptions and fostering placement, they also worked with those children who were emotionally handicapped/challenged. And they did this for the entire country. I was amazed to see how some of the children without limbs were actually attempting to participate in physical activities. I even saw those without arms painting beautiful pictures using their lips and mouths to hold the brushes. These physically challenged children were not trapped in a never-ending cycle of depression, but were actively working to improve the quality of their lives.

Our fieldwork schedule was very organized and demanding. Part of our project assignment was to study how other societies that we were to visit functioned, and how their people lived and worked in comparison to those in Africa, especially in Uganda. So, each person was given work assignments to share cooperatively with residents in the different communities with which we interacted and to which we took field trips. Such communities were located not only in England but in other Western European countries as well, including France, Italy, Ireland, and, to a lesser extent, Spain.

We thoroughly enjoyed touring Ireland with its great stretches of green scenic landscapes. We were stationed at Balydehob in southern West Cook. Every day, we would fill up our stomachs on pot-roast ham with boiled white potatoes and cabbage. And we would joyfully end the day spending the evenings in a pub singing loudly as the older men drank their Guinness beers. I was both surprised and saddened that many of the younger generations were immigrating to the United States and leaving the older folks to work their farms alone. While there, we participated in the farm chores like milking the cows and harvesting the crops of potatoes and various kinds of fruit. But, let me tell you, we looked forward to our almost nightly pub visits. I observed that the local women spent the majority of their time at home doing housework and were not expected to go to the pubs in the evening. We were foreigners, so we were the exceptions.

In Paris, we were fascinated with historic sites like the Eiffel Tower, and the wide, well-constructed streets. We simply adored the gorgeously scented perfumes in the stores and the picturesque large citadels. We also admired the Versailles historical building and its fantastic flower gardens. We were able to tour inside of the building and found it to be a marvelous place. In Paris, it was difficult to find people who spoke English, even in the stores. So, we had a language barrier, but we were able to visit the "Romantic City." Members of my group often joked about how we did not see many people imitating the name of the city.

In Italy, we were thrilled to visit Rome because of the Vatican. On one Sunday morning, we saw the Pope when he showed up at the window to bless the crowds of people. We were told that we could use the phone there to "talk to God." But, none of us dared to do it. We thought that we might freeze to death or become immediately paralyzed on that kind of phone call! Today, I am sure they were referring to the Pope and not the Almighty God. After a short stay in Rome, we moved on to Calabria in southern Italy, where we stayed for another two weeks. Here, we enjoyed the cuisine. For example, we ate large dishes of cottage cheese as an appetizer, followed by a large plate of spaghetti or pasta as the main dish, with a glass of wine, as drinking water was hard to find. We loved trying to eat spaghetti like the local Italians who referred to us university students as "professors." We did not mind answering to that title, because it gave us VIP treatment and services. We got a kick out of the hundreds of Volkswagen cars we saw on the streets. They were everywhere; because they were so tiny, they could easily be squeezed and parked on the pavement as well as in the aisles in the middle of the street. So, when walking, one had to meander around the cars. Even though we had only one day in Spain, we were fascinated with the huge and scenic grape orchards and the wine-drinking. The architectural home styles were very pleasing to the eyes.

After each fieldtrip, we would return to the college, where we would have to complete certain academic requirements. We were obligated to submit a written paper about each visit and our experiences in the places we visited. Each individual paper had to reflect on what we saw, what we did, what we read, and what we heard and learned during those trips. It was tough but rewarding, because, in addition to all of the fun and amusement, we were required to present our paper to the class orally, followed by an open discussion. We were to incorporate our total experience into our presentation. At the end of my two-year program, I received a diploma in social development and social administration from the University College of Swansea. My diploma was signed by Mr. John Parry (the principal), and Mr. A. Lockhead (my professor), who was also the director of social administration courses. The diploma declared that on the basis of my coursework and successful examinations, I qualified for the diploma in social development, social policy and administration, individual and social psychology, principles and practice of government, economics of developing countries, principles and practice of social work, and sociology. It was such a wonderful international learning experience.

Of all the European countries we visited, I found England to be the most interesting, because I had read and heard a lot about its cultures and cities from those English-language records I had used to learn English in my youth. For example, I was already familiar with Oxford Street and Piccadilly Circus in London, the River Thames, Trafalgar Square, and Buckingham Palace. But now I got the chance to witness the Royal Changing of the Guards, and I got very close to the real Windsor Castle. So, when I actually visited these places, it was as if I had either been there or seen them before. Those English records had also taught me something about the British police department and how it functioned. I was impressed with how the UK civil and legal system encouraged its citizens not to argue with the policemen because it would be a waste of one's time. Interesting enough, I saw very few police officers in the United Kingdom on the streets or

Figure 17: UK graduation, 1964.

riding through the community. At the time, I had no idea that I would later find myself in a country—that is, the United States—where there were police cars at every street corner in some communities. Moreover, you only needed to make a telephone call to get them. I have also learned that sometimes when they are most needed, they are slow to arrive, given one's particular neighborhood.

Figure 18: UK International Night, 1963, I am second from the right.

Chapter 13

MY RETURN TO UGANDA, MY CHILDREN, AND THE IMPACT OF MY UK EXPERIENCE

When I returned to Uganda from the United Kingdom in 1964, I immediately realized how beneficial my experience in the United Kingdom would be for my career and my worldview. The trip had opened me up to a new world of possibilities. I had learned so much working with diverse peoples of various ages, because I was introduced to cultures and ways of life totally different from mine. However, the most precious reward of all was that I was given an opportunity to learn and to acquire diverse knowledge. At times, the scheduled workload was challenging and strenuous, but after its completion, I was successfully awarded my diploma. Oh, I was so proud of my accomplishment. Remember, too, I had been denied a primary and secondary formal education. I was to be neither seen nor heard.

When I returned to my home country, I even had a different attitude toward my growing children. I found myself more ready to listen to them with a greater depth of understanding. We started to operate in a more relaxed atmosphere when we conversed about growing-up issues. So, in my two years out of the country, I had learned the importance of handling my children's concerns with greater respect. They were to be seen, heard, and understood. Since each child was only experiencing normal developmental changes, I established a climate whereby we could come together and talk about anything. I lacked this communicative avenue when growing up and I feel that it short-changed me both emotionally and socially.

I also realized that it was very important that I show them the same compassion, respect, and unconditional love, if not more, that I showed the orphans placed under my care. Children need to experience outward expressions of love, like hugging and laughter, from their parents or caregivers. I also came to realize how important it was to make my children, as well as any child, feel that they could be trusted. So, with my newly discovered awareness, I was ready to give them my guidance instead of putting too many restrictions on them. Realizing that I had changed, my five children, who still thought I was too strict, felt freer to discuss their problems with me. So, we were now able to help each other. We would talk and talk and talk. We also had much more fun together, the six of us. Unlike me, my children would grow up realizing the importance of building up one's self-esteem. I vowed to myself that their childhoods would be different from mine. We became a close-knit family, but unlike my father's, ours was full of demonstrative love.

From the outside, we appeared to be well-off. In fact, some friends and relatives told me later that they never realized that we had any hardships because we always looked happy and content. And, they thought I had lots of money to afford such nice clothes for my children. What they did not know was that I used to make all the clothes for my children myself. I enjoyed sewing and decorating their clothes. I had no sewing machine, so I did all of my sewing by hand with a needle and thread. I enjoyed both needlework and crocheting. I took great pride in my children, and sewing for them was my favorite hobby. I was so glad that I had, as a child in my father's house, learned how to make my own sweaters. For this reason, I found it easy when it came to making outfits and sweaters for my own children, especially during the years following World War II, when everything was costly and scarce. I also taught my girls how to sew simply styled dresses as a way of instilling in them that with the right skills, they, too, could improve their lives, even if they had very little money. So, instead of groaning about what we did not have, we laughed a lot. And, since God always provided for us, we had faith that we would always be able to handle any family situations.

When I went abroad to study in the United Kingdom, it was hard to leave my children, whose ages ranged from seven to twelve. I did not want to leave them without sufficient financial support to keep them in school while I was away. But, interestingly enough, when I finally decided that I was definitely going, God quickly came through with a tremendous blessing. The medium for this blessing was a very kind American lady who was working with the Save the Children Fund (SCF), established in Uganda in the 1950s. Since we both worked in agencies devoted to children, she had heard of my need. Her response was nothing short of a miracle. Many people say *no* to God when He calls on them to help others, but this precious American found us a sponsor, a Canadian from Columbia, who agreed to support my family for the two years I would be away. This Canadian family sent my household fifty U.S. dollars for each child every three months. This money went a long way in Ugandan. So, my financial contribution and their fifty dollars to each child every three months made it possible for my children to remain in school while I was away. While in the United Kingdom for two years, I did not receive my salary from SBH, but I did get an allowance from the government of Uganda. My salary at SBH had been based on contributions and donations, since SBH was a nongovernmental organization. So, while I was away, such monies were used to pay my temporary replacement. My housing privileges were also assigned to the person who was hired as acting Deputy Administrator. So, my children lived with my relatives and Yona's relatives during the school holidays or other vacations from their boarding schools. The generous offer from the Canadian family ended once I returned. We owe much to this family because they played a great role in the type of people we are today. It was against policy for us to have direct contact with our donors. This was done so the recipients would not try to ask for additional services or more money. So, the denial of direct contact was designed to avoid the temptation of asking for more than offered. And, again, once the sponsored family gets on their feet, the case is closed. Our appreciation for their Christian act of kindness will forever bring warmth to our hearts.

This Canadian family had no biological or marital ties to us, but they did for us what some of our family members chose not to do. There were even a few incidents when some of my relatives were unnecessarily mean to me after they heard that I had tried to look for financial assistance. These relatives informed me that I should not have had so many children when I knew that I was not going to be able to afford to care for them. Then, to make matters worse, soon after my return, I learned that Yona was living in Masaka at his birthplace, unemployed and not able to work because of his alcoholism.

Over the years, some family members continued to criticize many of my life choices. However, at that time, they made no mention of the fact that I was literally forced to become a single parent. I also remember another time when unkind remarks from a relative upset my kids and me. This male relative wanted to know why I expected my children to go to the same schools as the children of the university principal. He continued by saying, "Gee! Your children should only do two years of high school or less, and then look for a clerical job [a filing job] in somebody's office." Remember, I had four girls and one son. I felt that the cultural belief of not wasting a formal education on females was being laced with bad wishes in an effort to undermine my decision to educate fully my girls as well as my son. We six decided to distance ourselves from such family members, because we did not want such attitudes to undermine our faith for the bright future we each envisioned for each other. We decided to do the best we could with the little we had. I praise the Almighty God for never leaving our side. My children continued to work hard in school, because they were determined to succeed by doing their best. What my disagreeing relatives never realized was the major reason I put all my children in boarding school. It was the only way I could be sure that they would have good meals every day with a glass of milk. In all honesty, I was unable to provide them with those basics at home. Believe it or not, there was one time when they returned to school for a new semester and found that an anonymous friend from our church had paid a full year's tuition for my youngest daughter, Damali. Each of my girls went to school when she turned seven years old, and I later sent all of my girls to one of the best schools in Uganda, Gayaza High School. This did not mean that we were able to afford the fees, but once they were accepted, I could not pass up the opportunity for them to be educated in such a prestigious academic institution. So, since it was by God's grace that they were even accepted, I knew that by grace the funds to pay the school fees would come, too. And I was usually allowed to make special arrangements to meet the payments. This particular boarding school was equipped with a primary-school section and then continued through the twelfth grade. The required uniforms were made at the school at a cost. I also made sure that my only son attended King's College Budo. Yes, God has been good to us as a family. I also thank God that we as a family can talk about our tough past experiences with laughter and with a sense that we have proven ourselves strong and thankful for each other.

Chapter 14

THE END OF COLONIALISM AND MY NEW POSITION AT SBH

To be honest, I have never been one to be openly engaged in outward political protest. Even though I was born and grew up under formal British colonialism, which lasted roughly from 1894 to October 9, 1962, I was not always conscious of my country's political reality or history. The early history of my country is linked to several kingdoms that include Bunyoro, Buganda, Ankole, and Toro, which may date back thousands of years. When visitors from England arrived in the area, they were very impressed with the sophisticated social and political orders of these kingdoms. This has already been explained in the introduction, but for the purpose of continuity in this chapter, I will repeat relevant information. Some of these European visitors even likened these organized African kingdoms to the feudal monarchies of medieval Europe. Once the British completely took over, they integrated the ruling classes of the kingdoms into a system of indirect rule, the idea of ruling through the former African rulers under the direction of the British colonial officials. The group that benefited the most economically and educationally was the Baganda, due to their agricultural economic lifestyle and their proximity to the colonial headquarters. So, in many respects, everything on the surface looked as if the Africans were still in control. Even the name of the country, Uganda, might have been a British corrupted version of the word *Buganda*.

Colonialism is an interesting phenomenon. One can be born and live under a foreign colonial power and authority and not be conscious of its impact on one's life. This is especially true when the type of colonial policy is indirect rule. For me, it was almost surreal, because most of my social interactions were still with fellow Ugandans. I rarely interacted with the Europeans because they were not part of my daily existence. So, I did not see them affecting my life in any large way. In a similar fashion, I do not remember being that concerned with the political changes that were taking place in the late 1950s and early 1960s until it began clear that the British governor was planning to step down and was preparing Sir Frederick Mutesa II, the Kabaka of Buganda, to take over, not as the governor, which was the title of the British authority that was stationed in Uganda, but as the president. I did not fully understand all that was happening, nor was I overly concerned. In fact, I was more focused on my upcoming trip to the United Kingdom. I was not totally oblivious to the fact that colonialism was not for the benefit of the Africans. I did not fully understand why the British took over our country, but I did recognize and understand some of the inequalities of the colonial system. Africans were usually employed in less-prestigious and low-paying civil-service jobs. This had been my father's situation. And, even though there were African chiefs employed in the colonial government, they had to answer to the Europeans. Even in the police force, there were both English and Africans, but the British held the top positions. Economically, emphasis was put on cash crops that were to be grown and harvested by Africans, but most of the profits went to our colonial masters while the majority of the people struggled to pay the colonial government all of the demanded taxes. Up until this day, I have not fully understood what the British came to teach us.

So, when I returned to Uganda from the United Kingdom in 1964, I returned to a new and colonialism-free Uganda. I was not in the country when independence was granted, but I got the opportunity to experience it through the eyes of my son Michael, who was about thirteen years old at the time. In one of his letters to me, he included drawings of the country's new original crest, the official insignia/coat of arms, the new flag of Uganda, and helicopters that were flying over the celebrations. Michael wrote: "I enjoyed the Independence Celebration very much … and the floats were very interesting … Betty Kibukamusoke was on a float as a brownie … On the 8th of October, the Union Jack had to go down and the Uganda National Flag had to fly in the air and when it went up whistles were blowing, people shouted and fireworks exploded and the town of Kampala is now called a city, and all the airplanes, which had come to Kampala, flew over the place at the same time … On the 9th of October, the Duke of Kent gave full Independence to Uganda, stating, 'I leave the country to you.'" So, when I arrived back home in 1964, I could see that the local people were happy to be independent, but it was obvious that there was some politically and ethnically based hostilities as well as religious strife and competition that were increasing on a daily basis.

When I went back to my job at SBH upon my return, I was appointed the Administrative Director of SBH since the previous administrator, Sylvia Gaster, was retiring and returning to England. Joyce Bulera was hired as my deputy administrator. I thought to myself, *How do I count all of the blessings from the Lord that I have received over the years?* He was always on time. When my children and I moved to SBH in 1958, my children were very young. They loved the babies and always volunteered to play with them in the yard and to babysit the little ones. My kids even took it as one of their hobbies during school holidays or whenever they were home. I also encouraged them to volunteer their time and their caregiving skills. It was no wonder that some of the orphan babies used to look upon my girls as their sisters and my son as their brother.

Now head of the orphanage, I worked hand-in-hand with other childcare agencies in the country and around the world. I also had lots of friends from all parts of the globe who supported our work in a variety of ways. Some sent parcels and packages of food, dried milk, blankets, including knitted blankets, and all kinds of clothing, as well as actual checks. The World Council of Churches, as a way of reaching out to needy children, made donations in kind as well as in money. Many of our worldwide friends also became sponsors of our orphaned children after we placed them in foster homes. We had lots of contact on a regular basis from our supporters in the United States, Canada, New Zealand, Australia, England, Norway, Germany, and Denmark, in addition to other countries.

Some of these countries also supported our needy children through the Save the Children Funds Sponsorship Program mentioned earlier. Other countries would send volunteers to Uganda for a certain period of time, usually for two years, to provide practical services. Such volunteers, especially those from Norway and the U.S. Peace Corps served as a great asset to SBH. Up until 1973, my home or residence at SBH was among the few homes selected to host the few U.S. Peace Corps volunteers who came to Uganda. We used to accommodate two of them every two years. SBH's responsibility was to provide them with good meals and suitable living accommodations. These young people greatly assisted SBH with their areas of expertise and diverse skills. And their financial contributions for their accommodations provided additional revenue for the upkeep of SBH. These young Americans usually provided excellent services; we valued their presence, and they made a real contribution to our work. We also appreciated the local citizens who generously offered their homes to host SBH children during the times of pending court decisions for permanent placement. Their help was invaluable. The visibility of the First Ladies of the country at SBH was also very much appreciated. For example, Mrs. Obote used to visit on the big event days since she was the president's wife. It gave the impression that the government was supportive of the orphanage's mission.

Around 1971, in the seventh year of my administrator leadership, I was offered another government scholarship designed to further my professional development. On this scholarship, I went to the United States to take courses relating to childcare practices. So, I enrolled as a student at Case Western University in Ohio. This university organized my individual program to be affiliated with Planned Parenthood in New York City. As part of my coursework, I was assigned to work with Planned Parenthood in four districts or boroughs of New York City—the Bronx, Queens, Brooklyn, and Manhattan. During my seven-month stay in the United States in 1971, I lived at St. Henry's Settlement in Brooklyn. I thoroughly benefited professionally from this

Figure 19: Reverend Canon Benon Lwanga (one of the oldest offspring of SBH) escorting Miria Obote, the former First Lady.

short study tour. However, I found it difficult to complete my final report. In this required report, I had to discuss the best way to implement and integrate what I had learned in such a way as to improve childcare services and agencies in Uganda. Producing this report was to be a monumental task because I had to compare and contrast such services and agencies in both countries. The United States was so vast and New York City, the "Big Apple," was so massive with its captivating islands, but I did my best. In order to fulfill my course requirements, which dictated that I go back and forth to my fieldwork assignments at the Planned Parenthood offices in the different boroughs, I had to conquer the New York City subway system. Imagine me, Faith Alexandra Kamya Nasolo Mulira, cruising the "Big Apple" by subway when as a child I did not want to board a public bus with strangers. But now, I was free-flowing, open to learn, and anxious to try new things, because I also knew that my children were being taken care of. While in New York City, my children were at their boarding schools, and they returned to SBH only during school holidays.

I always tried to implement new, innovative ways to improve the efficiency of SBH by incorporating more efficient ways of doing things that I had learned from my coursework and travels. So, when I returned to Kampala from New York, I continued to share my newly acquired knowledge with the staff at SBH, and I even established several satellite homes in remote parts of Uganda. When I retired from SBH in 1975, after some sixteen years of employment, I was so proud of my accomplishments. I can honestly say that with the help of international donations, I committed my energies to developing SBH into an organization that provided the very best care for the orphans and the best training program for nursery-care professionals in all of Uganda. Today, SBH is thriving, and its offspring mingle with and are accepted as members of the general society. It is such an inspiration and quite an experience to have watched this positive social change, especially in a developing country. Anyone interested in SBH who would like to make a financial contribution, sponsor a child, organize a visit to the home, or physically volunteer their time is much appreciated. The Web site is www.sanyubabieshome.com. At present, social workers continue to take very seriously their responsibility as advocates for the orphaned children, and they continuously work to convince the public of the importance of accepting orphan children as full members of their societies. Several of SBH children continue to be like members of my extended family. To them, I am still Maama Faith.

Chapter 15

MY HOUSE AND POLITICAL UNREST DURING THE OBOTE AND AMIN ERAS

As my children started to graduate from high school, I began to seriously consider making plans to leave Uganda. Sanyu completed high school in 1967, Michael in 1969, Mabel in 1970, Irene in 1971, and Damali in 1972. The economic and political situations were getting worse by the day. There was no longer any real security in the country. People were disappearing and being found dead, but no criminals were being brought to trial. People would be picked up from their homes or jobs by the security forces, never to be seen again. Under Idi Amin, this was happening to people in high-profile positions with great frequency. It was as if a violent war had been unleashed on those successful Ugandans and anyone else who was viewed as opposing the military government.

Idi Amin Dada (1925–2003) came to power on January 25, 1971, after launching a successful *coup d'état* against the then-president Milton Obote, who escaped to Tanzania. Ironically, Obote himself had seized the presidency by ousting, in February of 1966, President Mutesa II, who went into exile. And Obote had done this with the help of his army commander, Idi Amin, and the military. There were so many atrocities that took place under Idi Amin that it is impossible to speak of them in detail. But there were also a lot of terrible things that happened under Obote, who was president of Uganda from 1966 to 1971 and again from 1979 to 1985. I remember in the mid-1960s when my brother Douglas was arrested and put in Luzira Prison. He was accused of having said the "wrong words" about the president of the country, in a country where there was no freedom of speech. To keep my brother alive, I knew someone had to do something. So, I went to President Obote's office to present my request, but was informed that the president wanted me to put my request in writing, which I did. In reply to my written request, he sent me a message that my brother would be released that day and that I should go to the prison and pick him up. I went to Luzira Prison—a very scary place to go to—and I found him outside waiting for me. At that moment, I did not think about the violence and the inequalities of the brutal government; I was simply grateful to President Obote and happy to see my brother alive.

President Obote, in order to further secure his dictatorial power, had planned to rid himself of Amin, but Amin got wind of Obote's plan and organized his own coup against the dictatorial government of Obote. I was there for most of his reign, and I know that in the beginning, there was lots of local support for President Amin because he had rid the country of an individual who was becoming a more ruthless dictator every day. President Obote had abolished the local kingdoms, including Buganda, so, everyone was hopeful that things would change for the better when Amin appointed himself president. For a while, even the British were supportive of him; after all, he was a veteran of the British King's African Rifles. However, it soon became very clear that Amin was not "the people's deliverer." He tended to associate more with the Muslims and his own ethnic group, the Kakwa. The British, too, became unhappy with his leadership when he decided to expel the large East Indian population, most of whom held British passports. Amin was displeased that during colonialism, the Asian population had been given favor by the colonial government and had prospered economically because of it. For example, the

Europeans had been placed at the top of the society, followed by the Asians, with the Africans at the bottom of the social ladder. It is locally said that Amin offered the Asians the opportunity to stay and become Ugandan citizens, but they chose to leave.

It is also believed by many Ugandans that Amin and his special organized squads killed thousands during his seven-year reign from 1971 to 1979. He started first with the Obote supporters, then the Christians, and then the educated elite. There were so many prominent Ugandans who lost their lives, including the High Court Judge, Chief Justice Benedicto Kiwanuka; the vice chancellor of Makerere University, Frank Kalimuzo; Archbishop Junani Luwun; and, even one of Amin's wives, Sarah Amin. During the times of less violence and chaos, I had gone to see her to request support for SBH, and Sarah had responded very favorably to my request. In fact, she donated materials to build us a chicken shelter for five hundred chickens and gave us ten bags of chicken feed. As a result of her assistance, we were able to get plenty of eggs for the babies in SBH. However, Sarah and I never worked together again. She was found dismembered, and up until this present moment, her murder has not been officially solved or vindicated.

Unbeknownst to many outsiders, President Amin would also voice nationalistic ideas and deliver speeches on African pride in the area of hairstyles and dress codes. It is also important to note that in some instances, the army, during both the Obote and Amin presidencies, acted on their own without any direct orders from their commander-in-chief. Interestingly enough, under Obote, my life was threatened emotionally on a daily basis, but under Idi Amin, it was more physically threatened, because of the uncontrolled violence toward civilians every minute of the day and night by men in the military. Therefore, many of us realized that to survive, we would have to plan an escape route. But at the same time, I wanted to build a home in case my children and I returned someday to live. To do this, I knew that I would have to expedite my plans for safety reasons. The pressure was unbelievable. Would I survive long enough to accomplish this, or should I simply leave the country now? In the past, just the expected cost of such a project had deterred me, but I now decided to do my best to put forward my plan in what little time I had left.

An opportunity to embark on my plan had come some years earlier with a call from my brother Paul in the late 1960s. He said, "Hey, you talked about building a house for yourself, how far have you gotten with it? I have a customer in my office that needs some funds. This man cannot secure a bank loan, so, he must put some of his property on the market. He has a block-making machine that he is selling at a very low price. Why don't you come and get it before someone else takes it? Surely, you can make your own building blocks on the site." I was so excited because this would be an easier way to start the process of building my own house. Now, up to that point, I had made no real plans to purchase the land on which to build the house. But I was determined to build a house, so I bought the machine. My head was spinning from trying to figure out how all of this was going to pan out. Paul also gave me some suggestions on where to get financing. At first, I was consumed with how I was going to pay back a bank loan or any other type of loan with all of my financial obligations. But, after talking to supportive family and church friends, I finally secured a loan of 4000 Ugandan shillings, which was equivalent at the time to about 240 U.S. dollars. This was enough to purchase a three-quarter-acre lot of land in 1965 from the Kampala City Council. This was prime real estate located in the community of Port Bell, Luzira, which is beautifully situated with a view of Lake Victoria. I made arrangements to repay the loan in monthly installments. In addition, I had to acquire funds to purchase the building materials like cement, roofing, and so forth. This was a major endeavor. It was going to be very expensive and time-consuming, but "the six of us" were determined. After much reflection, I thought it best to send the children to the United States as a way to lessen my day-to-day living expenses and responsibilities. I had to focus. So, I sent them one by one. Sanyu went in 1968; Mabel in 1972; Michael in 1974; and then Irene and Damali in 1976. At the time, an old friend of one of my brothers named Steven Nagenda owned an airline agency. After explaining to Steven my urgent need to purchase airline tickets for my children to travel abroad, he allowed me to purchase their tickets and to pay him in installments. Needless to say, for many years, I was paying Steven monthly installments.

You may ask, why send the children to the United States and not the United Kingdom or to another country in Africa? When the Peace Corps workers lived with us at SBH, my children listened to their stories about America, and they viewed their photographs of sites in America well into the night on a regular basis. In discussions with these young Americans, my children heard about educational and employment opportunities in America. Furthermore, they were encouraged by these Americans to pursue a future in the United States. My oldest daughter, Sanyu, begged me to let her go to the United States for her higher education. Since graduating from high school, she had been so dissatisfied and disillusioned with life in Uganda. Sanyu was born a very independent person, and after living with the Americans at our home, she was convinced that the United States was the place to go. To facilitate this, she joined the Up With People (UWP) group when they visited Uganda in the later 1960s. UWP was started in the United States in 1965. It was founded by J. Blanton Belk as a positive voice for young people and went international in 1968. Sanyu toured with them to places in the United States and to several other countries before members of its leadership assisted in her admissions to the University of Hartford where she obtained a full four-year academic scholarship. The UWP also found her a nice American host family in Hartford in 1968, Carl and Marjorie Henry, who were marvelous, kind, generous people. Sanyu stayed with them whenever she was on break from school. My daughter babysat for them and lived with them as a member of their family. Later, Sanyu assisted me by making arrangements for her siblings to follow her to the United States. She also assisted her sisters in their admissions to either the University of Hartford or Hartford College for Women. All of my girls secured either a full or partial scholarship to these institutions of higher learning. They also worked in order to earn pocket money needed to help pay for the remaining part of their tuition fees as well as for personal expenses. They each worked hard, because I was not able to send them any financial support from Uganda due to the political and economic restrictions and limitations we had at the time. For all of these reasons, the kids were sent to the United States.

Yes, I had a lot of things going on, but I was still proceeding with the house. Earlier, I had drawn a sketch of what my future home would look like. It would have a porch in front of the house, three bedrooms, two full baths, a kitchen/dining room, a living room, a small room for storage, a pantry and a tiny linen room, a laundry room, and a garage for a car that I didn't have yet. In the back of the main house, there would be two one-bedroom apartments—one for a gardener and the other for a mother's helper. It was as if I was being divinely guided, the image was so clear. So, I started to confess, orally and firmly, "Hey, this is it. I'm going to go ahead and do it." I also prayed, "Oh God, please let me do it. Help me." And, indeed, as I held on to my confession of faith, "God the Almighty did it for me." It was as if Habakkuk 2:2–3 in the King James Bible had leaped off the page and grabbed ahold of me and my vision. For those who are unfamiliar with this scripture, it reads:

> Then the Lord answered me and said:
> Write the vision
> And make it plain on tablets,
> That he may run who reads it.
> For the vision is yet for an appointed time,
> But at the end it will speak, and it will not lie.
> Though it tarries, wait for it,
> Because it will surely come,
> It will not tarry.

I quietly started to collect the materials required to make the concrete blocks as well as the labor force. And in 1973, I started to build my house. I hired three men whom I supervised, and we embarked on the project together. On the site, there was no water supply. In fact, I had to hire three more men to fetch water from the nearest well one mile away. It was not only fun making the homemade blocks, but far less expensive than purchasing them. As soon as we had made a large number of blocks, we dug the foundation for the house and then started on the actual construction. We dared not make all of the bricks at once for the same reason that we left no building materials lying around on the site: The army soldiers were notorious for laying claim to people's movable property.

I used to invite some of my friends to come and have small house-warming parties on the site at each stage of the construction. They used to laugh at me and voiced their opinions that I would never finish the house, especially since I had a get-together/house-warming kind of celebration at each stage. In reality, these little house-warming celebrations turned the whole building business process of my house into a fun, communal activity which made it easier to deal with any and all of the obstacles I was still experiencing. The donation of their labor and their love and support were extremely needed and appreciated. It took me more than four years to complete the house. In fact, I left the country in 1977 before it was completed. However, it was finally completed in 1978 by my sister-in-law, Gera Mosha. I will always be grateful to her for this. Even to this day, I have never lived in the house for long periods of time. But it has oftentimes been used as a source of income, because I have rented or leased it out to international travelers from all over the world as well as travelers from other African countries. I only pray and hope that one day, members of my immediate family will be able to live in it when any one of us returns and finds it unoccupied. It is a reasonably nice-looking and good-sized house with a wide compound confined behind high walls and a strong gate. There are flowers planted around the house and enough land for a large garden. I feel confident that I have left behind an asset to be proud of and a memorial for my children and grandchildren to find when the time comes for anyone of them to return home to their motherland.

Figure 20a: My house at Port Bell, Luzira, with a view of Lake Victoria.

Figure 20b: My house at Port Bell, Luzira, adjacent to garden.

Chapter 16

MY STORE

One evening in the early 1970s, when I was still working at SBH, I heard a local radio announcement that ended up changing my life by providing me with a possible alternative or an additional economic opportunity. The announcer informed the public that all of the businesses being abandoned by the departing East Indians would now be available for qualifying local Africans to take over. Interesting enough and as previously mentioned, the British had continued to support Amin, who was a veteran of the British King's African Rifles, up until he expelled the 50,000 or so East Indians and redistributed a lot of their property to his co-conspirators. This Asian population was very entrenched in the economy of Uganda. So, Amin was not only displeased with their economic position, but also unhappy that they had been given favor by British colonials and had prospered because of it. It is said by many Ugandans that Amin was even more displeased when members of this group chose to leave after having been offered Ugandan citizenship if they stayed and helped to build a better Uganda. So, when I heard this radio announcement, I quickly thought of how I could use the money from a new business to purchase building materials for my house and to pay off some of the airline tickets I had bought on installment. Plus, I had to take care of the three children that were still in Uganda—Michael went to the United States in 1974, but Irene and Damali were still with me until 1976.

Interested persons were encouraged to complete an application, and then, if accepted, they would be called in for an interview. Since I had the time, I took the opportunity to apply. The names of those whose applications had been approved were later printed in the local newspaper. I was ecstatic when I saw my name—me, Faith Mulira! I had passed the initial screening. What was left was passing the interview. I was very apprehensive because the final decision rested with the government—the military government under Idi Amin Dada. My interview went well, and I ended up with a grocery store. Interview questions centered around the applicants' experience in handling money, how much they had in the bank, and their experiences working with people. There was no fee to pay because the store was allocated free of charge. At the time, stores were assigned only to selected individuals who had positive interviews and who the government agent thought would be able to manage the business successfully. I got the store in 1972, but it did not open until 1973. When it first opened, my nephews ran it for me; however, I was soon informed by a government representative that it was compulsory that I run the business on a full-time basis since it had been allocated to me. So, I had no choice but to retire immediately from SBH. Once I retired in 1975 from SBH, I had to also find a new place to live, and since I had just acquired the store along with all of my other financial responsibilities, I had little cash. So, I was really happy when a friend who lived in Bunamwaya, located off of the Kampala-Entebbe road, allowed me to come and live with her. And, even though I was a staff nurse by profession, I did not seek such employment again in Uganda because I had the store to run and to supervise.

I was eager to make my business pay off, especially since it was now my true source of income. I was able to secure a loan from what was then the Libyan Arab Bank. I was so grateful that the loan was approved immediately after I presented a letter of recommendation from my former employer. I worked very hard to bring the store, which had been terribly neglected, up to standard. It was tough, but I was determined. It was necessary to have the shop renovated and painted because it had not only been looted of its goods but badly damaged structurally as well. In other words, I had to start from scratch. After about a year, we were ready to open the store, which was located near the Mengo Hospital grounds and the army headquarters. I named the store Namagala-Nakasi Grocery Store after my mother because I wanted to honor her.

All of the supplies and most of the repair building materials had to be brought in from Kenya. Unfortunately, by the time the merchandise reached the shop, the cost had at least doubled. I also had to pay the import taxes, and, if one wanted to live, one also had to pay bribes demanded by the army soldiers as well as the customs officers and the border authorities at any and all of the road blocks. Therefore, my overhead was extremely high. So, in order to make any kind of profit, I had to raise the prices of my merchandise. But, when I did this, I was accused of overpricing my merchandise and was arrested at least three times at gunpoint by the army soldiers. I was found guilty of overcharging for petty goods, and I had to pay a large sum of money to be released. Of course, I was not guilty the three times that I was arrested, but the soldiers were looking for money. So, in order for them to let me go, I had to pay them something.

I had managed to stock the store with all of the basic products, and, for a while, my business was running normally. In fact, it was very successful until the army soldiers started to threaten me. The political corruption and the loose cannons among the soldiers made life very dangerous, especially for those individuals who seemed to be doing well. People were disappearing at a more alarming rate. I began to think of how many friends, acquaintances, and family members I had lost under the then present government. There was one shocking incident that would often come to my mind that took place while I was in the United States on the 1971 government-sponsored trip to New York City. I was getting ready to return to Uganda when I remembered I had agreed to call a certain lady whose brother, Professor Siegel, was a lecturer at Makerere University. I met him at a social gathering, and when he learned that I was going to the United States, he made a request. At this meeting, he gave me his sister's phone number and asked that I call her and let her know that I had seen him and that he was okay. This was not an unusual request; people often sent messages and sometime packets to their family members living in the United States through others who were traveling there.

Human life in Uganda was now hard and insecure. And the entire country was becoming more lawless as the military government and the soldiers who upheld the government officials bullied the civilians. When I finally called his sister, I was not prepared for the news that she gave me. She told me that her brother was dead. "He is dead?" I asked in total shock and devastation. "Yes," she said. "He was killed by the army soldiers." "When?" I asked. "Last week," she said. I was so shocked that I was beside myself. In fact, I could hardly speak any more. I admired her strength and bravery as she continued to tell me the story. I nearly canceled my return ticket to Uganda. But, at the time, I had to report back to my work at the orphanage. When I arrived back in Uganda, the talk of Professor Siegel's death, a U.S. citizen who was killed by the soldiers, was the "buzz." I learned that he was partly burned alive! It took me several weeks to get enough courage to drive down the street pass the site where his said tragic accident took place, and it was a most terrifying moment for me. I made a point of never driving down that street again. His death remains another "official mystery." This was what it was like back in the late 1960s and early 1970s. By the mid-1970s, the violence had escalated.

There were two other incidents that made it totally clear that it was time to leave my motherland if I wanted to live without constant fear for my life and property. First of all, my neighbor was killed in the presence of his family. This neighbor and I were building our houses at the same time, but he completed his before me and had moved in. One evening, a few months later after moving in, he was shot and killed by army men. This was too close. I simply could not take any more. So, I accelerated my plans to leave the country. I went to the governmental office that issued traveling documents. I was given permission to go to Kenya with the stipulation that I was to return to Uganda in five days. I bought the ticket, packed a few clothes in a carry-on bag, and took off. My actual planned destination was the United States, where my children were, via London. So, I just walked out of my store as if I would return in two days or so. If I had made it known that I was really leaving in an attempt to escape the political unrest in the country, I might have lost my life. However, my brother-in-law, Stephen, took over the store, and it is believed that he was kidnapped and later killed by military men. Unfortunately, he has never been seen again. Once in Kenya, I got a hotel, but I only stayed in Kenya long enough to get my visa to the United Kingdom.

I lived temporarily in the United Kingdom for the next two years, 1977 to 1979, working in different hospitals in England. For example, I worked as a midwife at the Whipcross Hospital in Laytonstone, East London, United Kingdom. However, I could only be hired for the position of an aide on the ward or as a social-worker aide. I was a qualified nurse with lots of experience, but my training and work experiences were all associated with and in Uganda. This was very frustrating, especially since it lowered my earning power. To make ends meet, I also worked in a convenience store in East London, a neighborhood not too different from 125th Street in Harlem, New York, during my time off from the hospital. I wanted to have more opportunities to improve my life situation, so, I set my eyes on the United States, hoping that there would be more occupational and educational opportunities there. I, too, had listened to those Peace Corps workers I had hosted at SBH up until 1973. I had also heard their conversations concerning opportunities in America.

Figure 21: Working as a midwife aide at a hospital in London, 1978.

Chapter 17

LEAVING UGANDA WITH SAD MEMORIES

Leaving my motherland was also a very emotional experience. I had to leave a lot of loved ones behind, not because I really wanted to, but because the country had become unsafe to live in. The political instability made it almost impossible for most people to prosper in life. In fact, the main emphasis was on surviving. I lost many relatives and friends from 1966 to 1976, but I had not had the time to truly grieve. Of course, not all of my loses can be attributed to Amin's corrupted government. For example, during Milton Obote's second term as president of Uganda (1979–85), I lost two of my brothers. Douglas was killed at his home in Kawolo in the presence of his children in 1980, and Moses, a medical doctor, was killed in Fort Portal at an Easter party soon afterward in the presence of his wife and son. I was in the United States at this time, but I do know that neither brother was openly involved in politics, so most likely they were simply the random victims of violence by the military. There were other close relatives whose deaths were not the result of violence.

My mother Yunia died in 1968 at the approximate age of seventy-seven. She had a Christian burial ceremony and was interred in her family burial grounds in Kitagobwa. This was her wish. At the time of her death, she was a widow. Since she had lived most of her life in this rural district, she was not well-known in Kampala. Therefore, there were few attendees from Kampala at her funeral. After the burial services, lunch, as was the custom, was served to all who attended. A few days following her funeral, I went to tell my seventy-two-year-old father of her passing. At first, he kept silent, but then he asked me, "Who gave you the permission to put an announcement of your mother's death on the air? I, the husband, should be the one to do that." At that moment, I declined to respond to his remarks. But, I thought to myself, *Who is this man?* He had sent my mother away some forty years ago for reasons we children never knew. By whose authority was my father speaking? Underneath all of it, was there still love for my mother? I am proud to say that I was the primary caregiver for my elderly mother, and at times my ill husband, in their later days.

Some six years later, on April 24, 1974, I lost my former husband to alcoholism. I mentioned earlier that when I returned from the United Kingdom, Yona was living at his birth home in Masaka. He was no longer able to work, and he never officially remarried. The sickness had reached a very developed stage, though he was not yet forty-five years old. My heart grieved for him, but there was nothing I could do to help him. Yes, we were divorced, but he was still the father of my children and the first man I ever truly loved. He died at the age of fifty-six. While married, I was sometimes verbally and emotionally, but never physically, abused when he was drunk. In spite of all this, when sober, he was such a kind, loving person. And he loved his children, but was never able to take care of them. He was sick. We all believe, though, that he is with the Heavenly Father. We continue to be consoled by this. My two younger children, Irene and Damali, were still in Uganda when he passed. He had a comparatively large funeral and a decent service. He was buried at Gayaza-Masaka at a special burial place for the Mulira family. Three days after his funeral, I went to my father's house to let him know, because he did not attend the funeral. I was even more surprised that he made no response when I gave him the news. He just kept quiet; my husband's death and funeral were not important incidents in his life. In fact, he simply went on talking about other things of interest to him. My father had a similar reaction initially when I told him that Yunia had passed. Soon after Yona's death, I also discovered that he had sold all of our land. However, the new landowner did not want the house that was still situated on the land. So, I had the house pulled down, but I was later able to use some of the materials, such as the iron sheets, doors, and window frames, for my new house.

My father passed in 1976, just two years after Yona. He was eighty years old. By the time of his death, he had lived the last fifteen years, from 1961 to 1976, in his house alone. He and Elsie did not divorce, but went their separate ways. In fact, one of their sons bought her a small house in a suburb of Kampala, where she lived with one of her daughters who was unmarried at the time. It was tough for my father because no friends, relatives, or children could put up with him for long periods of time. Only two of my brothers seemed to have cared about him. These two went as far as to offer my father transportation with a paid driver to drive him wherever he wanted to go. It was sad but most of my siblings found themselves too busy with their own lives and careers to visit him on a regular basis. Occasionally, three of us girls visited him. In fact, we three made sure that a hot meal was taken to him with some regularity.

My father also cooked for himself. However, his dishes were usually nutritious, but tasteless and very difficult to look at. They were almost "discovery quests." For instance, he would combine rice, barley, beans, peas, nuts, fish, meat, chicken, and sweet potatoes all in one pot. Usually, he made a very large pot and would eat the dish until it was finished. It took a while, but we three eventually persuaded him to take the hot meals we prepared for him. In the end, he came not only to enjoy our meals, but to expect them. However, father being "Festo very Baada" felt compelled to voice openly that our cooking was still second-class.

Toward the end of his life, my father became very bitter that his other children kept themselves too busy to visit him on a regular basis. He also had some professional disappointments. As previously stated, my father was the only Ugandan working with the British people in the revenue department in Kampala as a cashier. But, in spite of his status and position at work, he was earning far less money than the British cashiers. His co-workers drove cars or motorcycles, while my father rode a bicycle for years. He bought his one and only car in 1944, when I was twenty years old. Later, he did draw a small pension, but not because he retired from this government department. In reality, he stepped down from his position in the British colonial government to accept a new appointment as the Minister of Finance in the Buganda Kingdom. This was a very important appointment. The promotion was a surprise to him because he never applied for the position. Unfortunately, his ability to emulate the British ways of working caused him not to mix well with those who worked for the government of the traditional Buganda Kingdom. So, after only three months, he was laid off without any benefits. Since he had voluntarily left his other job, he had also lost those benefits. He appealed to the colonial government to be rehired, but he had lost his appeal since he had quit his former position of his own accord. It was not a very happy ending after so many years of hard work. Fortunately, most of us were grown at the time, which made it possible for him to survive on his small pension.

Before dying, he spent a few days in Mulago Hospital, where my brother Moses was on staff as a medical doctor. However, my brother only found out that our father was in the same hospital on the morning that he died. Yes, our father was a very rigid and opinionated disciplinarian who aspired to be more European in some aspects of his life than Baganda. But, he was also our father and made many sacrifices for his family, and for that I think he should be honored in the memories of his children and other family members. He provided for sixteen children and three adults on very little. He is to be congratulated for his hard work and fortitude for helping to raise sixteen children.

When Elsie passed away some eight years later, in 1984, I was not in Uganda. In fact, I had been living in the United States for some five years. She was around seventy-five years old, and she had worked very hard throughout her marriage to my father, having a baby almost every year for some eighteen years. In her later life, she was very sickly, but she was fortunate to have some of her children very near to assist her. I do not think that she had lived with my father for any length of time since 1961.

Both she and my father, like my mother and Yona, had Christian funerals. However, Elsie and my father were laid to rest in the family burial grounds at Masooli, located some eight miles from Kampala on the Gayaza road, on land that I had previously donated, since my father's home near Makerere was in the city and there was no space for burial sites. Earlier on, I had purchased five acres of land at this site and donated half an acre to the family for burials. When I first purchased the land and set aside the half-acre, I was thinking about those family members who might not have their own burial site. But, it eventually became the entire family burial ground.

Despite my father's domineering temperament, many of his old friends, family members and associates attended his funeral. After all, he was "Festo, the bad guy." After his burial ceremony and internment, everybody went back to the house where they were served lunch. For both my father's and my mother's funerals, relatives and "real friends" kept vigil (wake) for two nights—one before and one after the burial—where they sang gospel songs all night long. Lots of family and close friends stayed both nights.

Chapter 18

SOME INTERESTING EXPERIENCES IN THE UNITED STATES OF AMERICA

When I arrived in the United States in 1979, I had high expectations for my future. However, I was not aware of the possible hindrance that my race might cause me. As I learned more about the history of race relations in the American society, I consciously decided that I would not be a casualty of the system. I would take charge of my life and I would decide how far I would go in life. After all, I had survived the regimes of Apollo Milton Obote and Idi Amin Dada, in addition to the cultural hindrances that wanted to limit who I could become and what I could accomplish in my lifetime. Furthermore, I was once the only female in Kampala driving a moped. Over the past thirty-one years that I have lived in the United States, I have had some interesting experiences. I have discovered that there are people who live in the United States but know very little about other cultures outside of the United States. First of all, many Americans think that Africa is a country instead of a continent. Second, there is little recognition of the location of the fifty-four independent countries on the second-largest continent in the world. Third, many Americans have no concept of the climatic, geographical, economic, social, political, religious, and cultural diversity that exist on this continent. No, Africa is not one big jungle. Of course, there has been some progress made in the awareness of Africa given that President Obama's father was from Kenya and was a member of the Luo ethnic group. However, I continue to answer endless questions posed by individuals I encounter from all walks of life. They are asked by people standing in line at the grocery store, at the post office, or in a bank. At first, they are attracted to my accent and oftentimes think I am Jamaican. Then, when I share that I am from Africa, many get very excited, and the questions become endless. Inquisitive questions also came from the elderly persons whom I later took care of, and from their family members. Old movies like *Tarzan* and then special programs on poverty in Africa, as well as other selected and sometimes biased reports on Africa, have fueled negative views of Africa. Sure, we have had our dictators, but no country anywhere in the world has had total perfection in their leadership. Then, too, most public schools in the United States still have very few if any permanent courses on the history of Africa.

The questions were usually centered on my experiences growing up and living in Africa. I always encouraged a conversation with them by responding to their questions with enthusiasm. Some of the elderly would ask the same questions over and over again. So, at times, I felt I could sing my answers even in my sleep. The frequency of certain questions served to bring back good and bad memories of the past. These questions and my answers to such questions provided an exchange of ideas and lifestyles as my friends and clients told me of their lives as well. I took advantage of such opportunities to learn new words, and sometimes even slang. I have included some examples of the questions asked by the young, the old, friends and patients alike, along with my responses.

"Your name is Faith? Who gave you that name?"
"My father."
"Oh! Is it an African name? It doesn't sound like an African name."
"Well, that is what my father called me on the day I was born."
"Hmmm! Interesting. You must have been ordained from the day you were born."

"Do you like it here? Of course you would not like to go back to Africa, would you?"
"Oh, yes, I would."
"Oh, how come? Now that you can live so comfortably here, you still want to go back?"
"Yes, I have lots of relatives there."
"But, you don't have nice clothes out there. Do you have nice clothes like the ones here?"
"Ummmm!"

"Do you see the wild animals around you all the time, and do they stay in your house?"
"No."

"How did you decide to come to Connecticut and not California or Texas?"
"Why do you think I should have gone to those particular states?"
"Oh, they are warmer. Your weather is very warm in Africa, isn't it?"
"Well, I didn't know the difference until I was in the states. My children were already in Connecticut. So, I landed here to join them."
"Is it not very warm in your country?
"Well, it is warm, but not humid."

"Do they come near your houses? I mean the lions, elephants, and snakes?"
"No, I never saw these animals near my home."
"Don't 'you people' live in the jungle?"
"No and I have never come across 'those people' who live in the jungle."
"Oh, so you have houses there like the ones we have here?"
"Yes, we have houses, too."
"How come I always thought you lived in a jungle? So, you never lived in a jungle?"
"Well, I don't know why you came to believe that I lived in a jungle."

Sometimes I would show those individuals who were asking me questions some photographs of my family members, my house in Uganda, and other interesting sites. Some samples of their responses and comments are included below:

"Oh, my, you know sometimes we are so ignorant about Africa," commented one elderly woman.
"Oh, oh look, so you have bathrooms. I can't believe you have indoor showers too."
"Oh, is this your house? Why are you here? I wouldn't have left my house like this to go to another country."
"I am glad to get to know somebody from Africa. Now I have a different picture from what I always had."

The most vivid of comments occurred when one lady, after looking at the photographs of my children, stated, "Oh, ooh! Look, so your children wore shoes when they were little." I could not believe it. Of course, there are many children and some adults in rural areas who go barefoot or wear flip-flops for a variety of reasons, but there was a stereotypic assumption in the statement. It is also true that many of the previous questions and some responses exhibited very stereotypic views of the African continent and those of African descent. And, at times, the questions and comments were degrading. However, I tried to not be overwhelmed with such comments but to take the opportunity to teach those who at least exhibited a desire to increase their knowledge about Africa. I always thought it important to let friends know that the political situation of a country can cause its citizens to flee for their physical safety. Such a situation can also result from high unemployment, which can cause additional everyday crises that make living very difficult in one's homeland.

Through discussions, I also found out how some of the negative stereotypic views had hindered the people of African descent who were born in the United States from being viewed as full citizens of the United States. At times, for example, I too was treated in a similar fashion. It was not until I spoke with a different accent that people distinguished me from local African Americans. It was then that I was viewed as being more acceptable, but still a novelty and an exception to the norm. Today, with the Africa Cable Station through Comcast in many North American households, maybe more people will develop more realistic views of Africa and her peoples. After all, according to modern-day anthropologists and archeologists, Africa is the cradle of the human species. It could be everybody's place of origin. There are even stories of creation which contend that the Biblical Garden of Eden can be found in Uganda. To God be the glory anyway.

Figure 22: Family photograph in the United States, 1979 (*Back row, left to right:* Damali, Mabel, Irene; *Front row, left to right:* Sanyu's ex-husband Alan, Sanyu with son Derrick, and me).

Figure 23: Family photograph in the United States, 1984 (*Back row, left to right:* Irene, Michael, Mabel; *Front row, left to right:* Sanyu and Derrick, me, and Damali with baby Kofi).

Chapter 19

RELIGION, MY FAITH, AND THE POWER OF PRAYER

When I grew up, there were several European missionary groups in Uganda and they were responsible for establishing the first Western-style schools in Uganda as well as building and running the first modern hospitals. The members of these groups were usually looked upon by many of the local people as people of religion who were kind and very helpful. We used to regard them as the people of God. At least, that is what they made us believe. I am sure that many of them were good, honest people, but others were not. I am very sure that some of them at the time worked with and shared the racist ideas of the colonial government. It is very important that one is able to separate the message from the carrier, in order not to miss the blessing that might be carried by a misbeliever. I remember when I was growing up that even though the missionaries tried to teach us about God and how we were all the same as God's children, they, as a group, continued to keep to themselves and to believe that we as Africans were fundamentally different from them, the Europeans. They always kept their distance from us and we were never allowed to really get too close. In other words, they were missionaries, the enlightened, and we were Africans, the "backward people." As time passed, some of the barriers were no longer visible, and some of the European missionaries and the Ugandans began to interact more on a basic human level. I do know that the genuine missionaries who had the real love of God within them were the best to live among and to trust.

I believe that the genuine ones continue to make a positive difference in the lives of the people in Uganda. Today, the churches, along with their leadership heads, and the congregations are only segregated according to their beliefs—Catholics, Muslims, Protestants, Seventh Day Adventists, and so forth. What was always surprising was that even though all of these denominations advocated love, they themselves were in conflict and in competition with one another for converts. Unfortunately, their hostile relationships sometimes spread over into their colonial converted communities, resulting in civil wars like the one in the 1890s between the African Protestant converts and the African Catholic converts in Uganda.

My father, who was a Protestant, attended St. Paul's Cathedral, which was, as I stated before, under the Church of Uganda, located at Namirembe. He did not have a special position in the church but was recognized as a regular member. Both he and Elsie belonged to the same faith and church. I am so thankful that he raised us as Christians. I was baptized when I was two and a half months old. After the baptism service at the church, there was a special cup of tea with bread and butter for the family. This was served following the baptism of all babies. As a family, we used to go to church every Sunday, walking some two and a half miles. All of us who were old enough to walk to Namirembe had to go. And, as mentioned in an earlier chapter, in my father's house, the reading of scripture and praying were done together early in the morning before any one of us left the house, and again in the evening before we went to bed. And then a prayer was said before every meal by one of the children in turn. As each child learned to read, he or she took turns in both praying and reading a scripture from the prayer book. My father made sure that each of us received our own personal prayer book at the appropriate time. Then, too, as a child, I often used my Bible to practice my English, as was suggested to my father by one of his European co-workers. So, I really grew up learning and reading about the Lord and his mercies regularly.

My birth mother, Yunia, was also a Christian. I remember how my mother used to take my youngest child, Damali, to worship services with her. From the age of three to the age of eleven, Damali had suffered from a kind of eye ailment. My mother used her faith in the healing power of God to assist Damali in receiving her healing for her eye problem. So, my mother used to travel by bus so that she could take her sick granddaughter to a gospel prayer meeting. From an early age, Damali loved going to these meetings and being with Grandma Nakasi. Damali would often start singing the gospel songs she learned while we were at the table eating. And none of us were able to stop her even when we tried. She would sing the entire song before stopping. Her most favorite songs spoke of God's awesome power, His sovereignty, and His greatness. Damali would always have such a peaceful expression on her face when singing these songs. It was as if she was in God's presence and clothed in His love.

My mother and Damali enjoyed going to the gospel prayer meetings, which used to be held in a high tent on the open grass. People from distant areas also came to these prayer meetings, or "camp meetings," as they are referred to in the United States. However, I think that most came for healing. The place was always packed, and the lines to receive prayers for healing were exceptionally long. The attendees would sing joyfully and loudly clap their hands. Many of them were also filled with the Holy Spirit with the evidence of speaking in tongues. Their songs of praise could be heard a long distance away, and the people who heard them knew these services were praising God.

Damali's eyes cleared up, and she has never suffered the ailment again. What is most interesting is that none of us can remember when they cleared up. The problem of her eyes went away unnoticed. She had been healed. This is something that Damali cannot forget about her Grandma Nakasi. There are many experiences in my life that attest to the power of prayer to heal. I will share with you several of the most important ones that I have experienced so far in my lifetime.

Healing and deliverance through the power of prayer is as real as life itself. However, it does require that we believe when we pray that we have received that which we have requested from our Lord and Savior Jesus Christ. In the following paragraph, I would like to share with you several of the many tremendous personal testimonies whereby I prayed, I believed, and I received that which I requested by faith. At times, it has been physical healing, and at other times, it has been deliverance from dangerous, life-threatening situations.

TESTIMONY #1

In 1956, I had severe hemorrhaging after suffering a miscarriage. I was alone in a foreign country without family support. As discussed in a previous chapter, I had gone to Kenya to work, leaving my husband and children in Uganda. I was fully conscious and aware that I was bleeding as a result of a miscarriage and that the situation was very serious. So, as my blood pressure continued to drop, I knew that I would die in my room alone without God's direct divine intervention. I prayed, requesting God to help me and to spare my life so that I might live and take care of my five children in Uganda. About four hours later, a co-worker returning from a business trip unexpectedly stopped by my house to inquire about the condition of the patients, only to find me in worse condition than the patients. Immediately, he had me rushed to a larger and better-equipped hospital some forty miles away for treatment. I could do nothing but pray and believe in my Lord and Savior to deliver me from a premature death. God indeed answered my prayer, and I miraculously survived.

TESTIMONY #2

Sometime between 1971 and 1978, I found myself faced with guns aimed at my chest by a gang of Idi Amin's soldiers. The soldiers, who had stopped me at a roadblock, accused me of not coming to a full stop quickly enough. They were speaking in Kiswahili, so I pretended not to understand what they were saying. With their guns pointed at me, they had only to pull the trigger to end my life in a flash. My blood pressure shot up so quickly because of my fear that I could hardly keep standing on my feet or raise my head. I called on God's name for help. I also looked in the eyes of one of the soldiers, the one that was on my side of the car. I just knew that he was going to shoot me at any time. So, I just loudly called on the name of Jesus Christ to help me. At that moment, the soldiers lowered their guns, and one said in Kiswahili, "Aya kwenda," which means, "Okay, you go." My deliverance from death by the hands of these soldiers was again by the grace of God. I had only escaped death through prayer and my faith in God that he would come to my rescue in a time of trouble. God also came to my rescue when I was arrested at gunpoint three times before I left the country in 1977.

TESTIMONY #3

In 1998, I was diagnosed with breast cancer. Interestingly enough, when my physician explained to me that the biopsy of the discovered lump was cancerous, I was not totally overwhelmed by the news. I listened as he explained his treatment plan. He stated that I would have surgery and afterward treatments of chemotherapy and radiology. Realizing that I had no control over the situation or diagnosis, the only thing left for me to do was pray, and pray hard. I asked God for his help and to give me the courage and confidence to go through this experience. I then went to my church, the African Methodist Episcopal (AME) Church in Bloomfield, Connecticut, and told my pastor, Reverend Alvan Johnson Jr., the news. Reverend Johnson immediately reached for the bottle of anointed oil to put some on my forehead, saying, "By His faithfulness, you will be okay." So, I was strong in my belief that God was in charge, because I was letting Him take charge of my life. On the scheduled day, I went into surgery as if I was going in for a minor cut-dressing. I had no fear because I felt myself clothed in the "power of prayer." In other words, I was fully convinced that God had taken care of the cancer.

The following day, after surgery, I was discharged from the hospital, and I was instructed to return to start my chemotherapy in a few weeks. Prior to my first chemotherapy treatment, I attended an orientation meeting with the oncology nurse. The orientation group members made me feel welcomed, comfortable, and secure. In fact, the orientation meeting was as if we were discussing preparations for a party. The members promoted hope not fear. To my surprise, my chemotherapy took only six months. All I can say is that I was being guided by God's love, grace, and protection. I did not suffer any side effects from either the chemotherapy or the radiology treatments. In the end, I was awarded a diploma as a cancer survivor. That was some twelve years ago. Think of that! God is good all the time. Hallelujah, hallelujah. All praise be to God. I also believe, as did the oncology staff team, that my positive attitude and faith in my Lord and Savior Jesus Christ helped to promote my quick recovery. So, as I was being awarded with a cancer-free certificate, I was praising God for His love and mercy.

TESTIMONY #4

A fourth healing through the power of prayer took place about two years after my breast-cancer surgery and recovery. As part of that surgery, some of the lymph nodes were removed from under my right arm. Initially, this had caused me some discomfort. Well, after about two years, the veins in my right arm began to hurt and tighten up, preventing me at times from being able to straighten out my arm. Even though I laid hands on it and prayed for healing, the arm seemed to be getting worse. So, I became somewhat worried, especially since it was the same arm from which I had had the lymph nodes removed. I knew that my increased worry was actually fear, which was countering my faith, causing it to be ineffective. How was I to be divinely healed when I was so bottled up with fear or simply disbelief in the manifestation of my healing? One Sunday when I went to church, the pastor invited all members of the congregation who had need of a special prayer to come to the altar. I joined the many others who came. The pastor and his team touched every single one of us and repeated a prayer for everyone who came up front for prayer. When my turn came, the pastor himself touched my forehead and started praying. I wanted him so desperately to touch those stretched veins, but there were so many people at the altar that I decided not to make that specific prayer request. So, when he touched my forehead while praying for me, I placed my left hand on the painful veins in my right arm. At that moment, I was not aware that healing had taken place. It was only after I had returned to my seat that I realized that my right arm was as normal as my left one. I cannot express the great feelings of jubilee that I experienced. The pain was gone and the veins had loosened. Up until this day, the ailment has never returned.

TESTIMONY #5

This fifth testimony is the one I believe to be my most miraculous example of healing through the power of prayer. It is important to read this example carefully and thoroughly. It will be a great blessing to you and a testimony of God's power and love. My second daughter, Mabel (who is also named Kirabo), and her husband had been married several years and really wanted to have a baby. All of my other children had had their children earlier in their marriages. I prayed a lot for them as a couple. At different times, I would go and kneel beside their bed in their bedroom when they were not home, and say a special prayer for God to bless them with a child. There were also times when we went to church together and we would go up to the altar for special prayers. During such times, I would touch my daughter's shoulder and pray silently for her. Well, God eventually answered my prayers. Mabel became pregnant; however, the baby was delivered six and a half months into the pregnancy, weighing only one and a half pounds. Their cute little child was named Kirabo after her mother, but also because the name itself means "a gift." And this tiny bundle was indeed both a miracle from God as well as a tangible gift from Him. Baby Kirabo was kept in the incubator in a neonatal intensive-care unit for some time at one of the best hospitals in Connecticut. I remember the nurses telling the father, Jerome, that the baby was the size of his palm but very cute. Baby Kirabo underwent several surgeries in an effort to assist her immature and weak organs to function more efficiently. I often made trips to the hospital to visit the baby. Even though she was very delicate, she would freely stretch her legs and arms. I could only view her through the window since only the parents were allowed to get very close in order to avoid any infection.

There were times when I would look at baby Kirabo and questioned God, saying "Lord, is this the baby you decided to give to my children, will she survive?" As I complained to Him, I did not hear a clear answer from the Almighty, but I think He said, "Yes, that is the baby I gave your children." When my daughter was discharged, she had to leave the baby since she was still less than five pounds. Mabel visited the baby every single day. She cherished this little blessing that God had given to her. She once told me that visiting each day was her therapy. As I continued to pray, I slowly regained my trust and faith. So, even during those times when doubt wanted to overtake me, I drew on the higher power within me. I recognized that God was still the Great and Almighty God, and that He was still in control and that baby Kirabo would cause Him to be glorified in our lives.

Once, when I returned from a month and a half out of the state, I found that baby Kirabo, the once-tiny baby, had grown into a normal baby of seven pounds. I could hardly believe my eyes. This was the grandchild whose survival I had doubted. After she was released from the hospital, she continued to grow at a normal rate. Today, she is twenty years old and a college student who wants to go to medical school. In 1999, Mabel was blessed with another daughter, Nakasi, whom she named after my mother. God is so great! The power of prayer works.

There are other incidents, but I cannot mention all of them in this book. I simply wanted to assure those reading this book that there is healing power through prayer. If we do not get the answer we expect from our prayers, there is always a reason for it. The answer may also come in a different form, because God may have something even better for you. You must always remember to pray that His will be done.

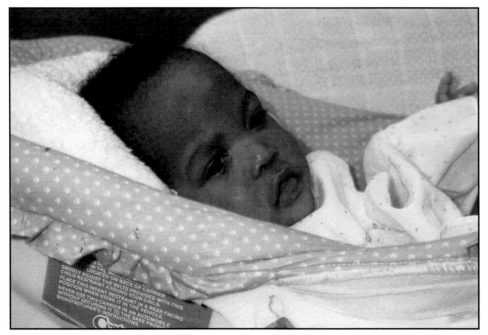

Figure 24: Baby Kirabo, at six months old.

Figure 25: Nakasi, Jerome, and Kirabo, 2010.

Figure 26a: Mabel and Jerome's wedding; Jerome's mother and me, 1983.

Figure 26b: Michael and I with the bride.

Chapter 20

A THORN IN MY HEART AND A CHALLENGE TO AGAPE LOVE

One October day in the early afternoon of 1989, I received a telephone call from my sister-in-law Olivia, who lived in London. She explained to me that my sister Evelyn, with whom I share the same father, and her husband, John, had been killed in a Ugandan plane crash in Rome. I was so shocked and beside myself that I shouted loudly, "No, no, please tell me this is not true!" It was too much for me to take in, so I dropped the phone and hung up. Olivia called back a minute later to confirm that both were reported to have died in the crash. In fact, we were initially informed that there were no survivors among those traveling to Uganda.

When I asked her what we could do, she informed me that our nephew, Michael, who also lived in London, had already flown to Rome seeking more information and to see if he could track down Evelyn's body. They assured us that Michael and his wife Hilary, as well as relatives in Uganda, would keep us informed by phone of any news of the incident. Later, Olivia did call with news that a few passengers who had been thrown some distance from the plane into the bushes had survived. The rescuers had heard them calling for help. Thanks to God, Evelyn was among those survivors that were picked up by the Red Cross ambulance and taken to one of a variety of hospitals in Rome. However, all of the dead had been collected and stored in a building somewhere, we had no idea where.

Michael had to be strong. He, led by the police, had initially gone through all of the bodies looking for both Evelyn and John. Unfortunately, he did locate John's body and later found Evelyn's pocketbook with her documents, but no body. So, he assumed that she might have survived. The mission now was to find the particular hospital to which she had been taken. At least with her documents he had a photo. Michael took advantage of the transportation that was provided for the relatives and friends searching for their kin. It took him a full day to locate Evelyn in the hospital. She was in great pain, both of her legs having been broken. She was still in her bloodstained clothes and was unable to respond to anybody. At last, Michael called and filled me in, and he said, "Aunt Faith, can you please come over, I cannot handle this alone." "Where are you?" I asked him. "Somewhere in Rome at a hospital." "Okay, I will call you back," I replied. "They said that Evelyn must undergo surgery," Michael said.

Two hours later, he called again to give me the name of the hospital and also to let me know that the Ugandan government was making arrangements to have an official representative at the airport in Rome. The representative would meet the victims' relatives and direct them to the location of their injured family members. This was all so surreal. I was busily moving but getting nowhere. It was as if my mind was on autopilot. My actions and behavior seemed to have been separated from my thoughts. I quickly found someone to cover my job while I took an unpaid leave. But, no matter how hard I tried, I could only get a visa and plane ticket for the following day. So, I arrived on the third day after the crash.

On arrival at the airport in Rome, I saw someone holding up a board with my name. This person then led me to the prearranged transportation that took me to the hotel that had also been arranged by the Ugandan government to accommodate all of us Ugandans. Because of the lateness of the hour, I was informed that

I would have to wait for the next day to see my sister. So, early the next morning, we were provided transportation to the various hospitals. These arrangements were of a great help since there was almost nobody who spoke English.

When I first saw my sister, I was overwhelmed with shock. Tears were running down my cheeks as I tried not to cry out aloud, not wanting to scare Evelyn. She was semiconscious, and both legs were in extension with strings and iron bars holding both legs up in the air. There was also a notice on her bed with instructions not to tell Evelyn of her husband's death until the hospital's social workers had spoken to Evelyn and her relatives. Fear gripped my heart when she would sporadically utter John's name. Maybe she wanted to know whether John survived, or she was calling him just to know if he was near her. We could not tell because she was not responding to anything unless one touched the ropes and instruments holding both of her legs in the air. She was in a very scary condition, and could only blink to indicate she was in pain. She was also on a twenty-four-hour intravenous drip.

We became more hopeful when we were given permission to give her a sip of water every so often. Two days after my arrival, the hospital workers began to deliver her light meals, which they often brought and left beside her bed regardless of whether there was anyone to feed her. The sipping of the water was a positive sign to us that progress was being made. God had also made sure that she had someone with her before any family arrived. For instance, before I arrived in Rome, a female co-worker friend of Evelyn's from London had come to Rome, after taking an unpaid leave, to be with Evelyn until somebody from the family could arrive. Unfortunately, I never got to meet her and to learn her name, because she left Rome just as I arrived. I often think about this great soul who allowed the Lord to provide my sister companionship. She was indeed an angel sent by God.

This was almost an unbearable situation, and it was made worse by the language barrier. It was always very difficult to find anyone who spoke English. Therefore, we had only minimum communication with the people around us, let alone the nursing and other medical staff. We were overjoyed when we learned that a Ugandan student, Reverend Joshua, studying at one of the seminaries, had agreed to assist with our communication challenges. He had agreed to go around the various hospitals and try to find out what we, non-Italian-speakers, needed so that he could inform the doctors and nursing staff of our needs. Unfortunately, Reverend Joshua could not get to every hospital each day. So, we were stuck until he came. The language problem even hindered us from getting our basic needs. For example, I was never able to find anyone to give me or show me where I could get hot water to wash Evelyn. So, I would use the hot water that came on the breakfast tray to wash Evelyn's face and other parts of the body. Then, I would take the teapot to beg for more hot water for her cup of tea. It was difficult because whenever I tried to get water, they would only give me coffee. There was always plenty of very strong coffee when there was neither water nor tea in the vicinity. Usually when I asked for water, I was offered either wine or coffee instead.

Reverend Joshua was indeed sent by the Almighty. One day, I requested that he ask Evelyn's doctor if she could be transferred to England. There, we had more relatives, we could all speak English, and we were familiar with the British system and how things functioned. Her doctor's immediate response was predictable. "You cannot find good doctors like the ones in Rome anywhere else." So, we continued to try and make the best of a difficult situation. Then, deliverance came in a phone call! About a week after the doctor's response, I was told that there was a person on the phone who wanted to speak to anyone who was with Evelyn. So, with hope and thanking God, I went to the phone, and lo and behold, it was a person from Evelyn's medical insurance. Oh, my God! I jumped for joy. Immediately, I poured out my problems and expressed to him that I preferred that my sister be transferred to London. He, too, repeated that "there are very good doctors in Rome." I begged him and replied, "Yes, I understand, but can the insurance please pay for her to be transferred to London?" He replied, "Well it could be done if that is what you want. Let me get back to you later."

About three hours later, the insurance representative informed me that we could make arrangements to have Evelyn transferred to London. However, we would need to hire a special small plane that would carry only four persons—Evelyn, the pilot, a nurse, and me. He explained that we must have a nurse but that he had not found one. I urged him to try harder to find one and if he was unable to do so, I was a nurse. Then, he asked me if I was registered as a nurse in the United Kingdom. When I explained that I was registered in Uganda, the insurance agent explained that I could not be hired for this position since I was not registered in the United Kingdom or in Italy. He further stated that he would get back to me as soon as he could. When he did call, he told me that his wife was a registered nurse in France and had agreed to accompany us on the aircraft. So, later in the afternoon, after having made all the transportation arrangements, including the ambulance ride from the London airport to the hospital, we were consumed with the possibility of a quicker recovery period for Evelyn in London. He also told me that I would find instructions at the hospital in London to direct me to a hotel where I would be staying until I was ready to return to the United States, and, furthermore, that an underground transportation station would let me off a short two blocks from the hospital.

I was filled with indescribable joy as I informed Evelyn that we were moving her to London the next day. I was not sure whether she heard and understood all that I was jabbering about. Nevertheless, I was filled with joy that we were leaving Rome. I had been in Rome for a week and a half, and each night I would have to return to the designated hotel and then use the bus to return to see Evelyn every morning. At times, the buses were either late or full. In fact, there were many times when I had to wait for another hour for the next bus, delaying my arrival at the hospital until 10:00 A.M. or later. During such times, I would always find Evelyn's breakfast tray beside her bed untouched. By the time I got someone to allow me to warm up everything, it would almost be lunchtime. We had to get out of there quickly. I felt the place was actually hindering my sister's recovery. When we got to London, where I stayed for another week, my nephew Michael and his wife Hilary were waiting for us. They provided me with a ride to the hospital, because I was not allowed to ride in the ambulance with Evelyn in London. After a few days in the hospital in London, Evelyn was sporadically able to participate in a conversation. After such progress, her doctors allowed us to tell my sister of her husband's death bit by bit. John was cremated about two weeks after his death. This was only a few days after Evelyn had been flown to the hospital in London.

On our second day in London, my other sister, Ndiwoza, arrived from Uganda to be with Evelyn. This sister had traveled halfway to Rome before she learned that our sister had been transferred to London. At that point, she was able to divert her route to London, arriving just before midnight. She was also put up in the same hotel as I. The next day, we visited Evelyn, and with tears in Ndiwoza's eyes, she started singing to Evelyn one of her favorite hymns from her personal prayer book, the book that was given to her by our father. The song is very spiritually uplifting and it spoke of faith in God, God's faithfulness, His love, and the ability of His Spirit to help those who trust in Him to overcome the challenging circumstances of life. The words of the song seemed not only to calm Evelyn but to provide her comfort. So, we sang it softly for a while until a tray was brought for lunch. That day, Evelyn seemed to enjoy the food, and it was, after all, familiar to her. The meal consisted of rice, beef, veggies, and a cup of milk. We were so surprised when all of a sudden Evelyn said, "I am enjoying what I eat." Boy! We were filled with joy. From that day onward, she continued to get better day by day.

On the day that her husband was cremated, we prepared Evelyn for it and talked to her about it. We tried to answer all of her questions and then said a prayer with her at the very time that the funeral was taking place. I had on occasion visited Evelyn and John at their residence in London. They were very loving toward each other. And they were such a happy couple. So, I was so heartbroken because Evelyn had lost not only a husband, but also a very good friend. After a week in London, I returned to the United States, leaving Ndiwoza with Evelyn. I called frequently to get updates on Evelyn's recovery. When she was discharged, she went home with John's parents. In fact, she owned an apartment located above her in-laws' apartment.

During one of our telephone conversations, Evelyn explained that she was so much better, and that her doctor was allowing her to start working part-time. This was good news to me because it meant that my sister was really going to be okay and able to take care of herself. So, I replied, "Oh my, that is nice. Thank God for it." At the time, Evelyn was downstairs with the in-laws, and she told me to hold on for a few minutes while she went to her own upstairs apartment to talk to me. I replied that I would gladly wait. Of course this was an expensive international call, but, hey, this was my sister whose life God had spared. To my surprise and bewilderment at the time, Evelyn never came back to the phone to speak with me. I waited and waited, and after some time, I hung up and called her again, but she never picked up. I called again the following day, but she still did not answer. I grew very concerned, so I called her in-laws, who explained that she was okay and that one of her nieces from Uganda was living with her.

This was my sister, whom I loved dearly. I continued to call, but nobody answered the phone or returned my calls. And you know what? She has never called or written to me since that time. I mean there has been no communication from her of any kind. Furthermore, whenever I go to Uganda, she avoids me. Later on, I learned from the people who were with her the last time that I spoke to her on the phone that she had gotten mad at me because I had praised God when she told me that her doctor had given her permission to work. She had thought, how could I praise God when I knew that her husband had just died? Yet she was alive with the breath of life. According to her, she no longer believed there was a God, because God would not have let her husband die. She failed to see God's blessings in her life and in her survival, which were obvious testimonies of His love for her.

She also told relatives that her nephew Michael and I had taken the trouble to come to Rome only because we wanted to share in her husband's insurance death benefits. In reality, I knew nothing about her husband's insurance benefits. The insurance representative I spoke with in Rome talked only of Evelyn's medical insurance when I requested that he have her transferred to London, but I never inquired about any financial benefits. In all honesty, I flew to Rome only to give loving support to my sister who had just survived a plane crash and who was in a state of shock and needed family support. I never expected any financial reimbursements. I was only pleased that I could be there for her and help her be transferred to London, where we had lots of relatives and acquaintances who could visit her and give her the continuous support she needed while recovering. In addition, in London, there were no longer any communicative challenges with the doctors and nursing staff.

I was hurt that my intentions to show my sister unconditional love were misunderstood. It felt like a thorn had pierced my heart. I was also disappointed that I was never given the opportunity to share with her the experiences that she and I went through while she was in the hospital in Rome and afterward. So, there is no way she will ever know or fully understand how it is God's grace that she is alive. Long after this sad event, I discovered that the Ugandan government had offered five hundred dollars each to any two relatives of the victims who had gone to Rome. I never even tried to claim this money. I willingly answered my nephew Michael's call for help. I did not even wait to hear what other relatives' plans were. Olivia, Michael, Hilary, and I were the closest to Rome, so we rushed to my sister's side to help. Today, I am extremely happy that my sister is alive and content. I still thank God and will always praise Him because I did all that I could do through Him, who strengthened me. I believe that when we do an act out of the goodness and the kindness of our hearts, without the expectation of a "natural" or physical reward, God sees it as a sacrificial offering to Him. I think that if Evelyn knew the levels of God's love for her, she might have had a different response to my comment about thanking God for being able to go back to work.

Chapter 21

THE ACQUISITION OF MORE EDUCATION AFTER MY SECOND ARRIVAL TO THE UNITED STATES

When I arrived in the United States in 1979, I was fifty-five years old, and I was so happy that I, too, had listened to those Peace Corps workers at SBH many years ago. They had opened my eyes to the possibilities of success in the United States. I had also noticed that most of the textbooks we used in our classes in the United Kingdom had been published in the United States. In addition, I was so impressed with the positive experiences of my children who had arrived in the United States some years earlier. My children had always taken school seriously, and all of my girls had graduated from college before I arrived. So, I found them graduates who were already employed in jobs for which they had been recruited while attending college. I was so impressed that they had taken advantage of the educational and economic opportunities in America.

So, my choice to immigrate to the United States as opposed to Europe was threefold. First, my children were all living in the United States. Second, I was seeking physical safety in a less conservative society. Third, I thought that the United States would provide me with more opportunities to learn and to enhance the quality of my life. Now that I had personal and physical security, I embarked on the acquisition of additional knowledge so as to become more marketable. I needed to be able to take care of myself, and given my age, I quickly realized that any job in the U.S. nursing field, with the exception of a nursing aide, would eventually require more education. I truly believe that there is always a way for an individual to improve his or her life circumstances. The key for me has been my willingness to learn, which has allowed me to take advantage of any and all opportunities that have come my way.

Other aspects of my personality, like my determination to succeed in life, my hardworking work ethic, and my policy always to learn something from whatever situation I have found myself in have proven to be very beneficial. Throughout my life experiences, whether pleasant or unpleasant, I have embraced the opportunity to learn, and I consider this to be one of my greatest attributes. And I know, without a doubt, that all of my educational achievements, including my degrees, licenses, and certificates, are the result of hard work, personal sacrifice, and God's help. Take my learning of the English language. I grew up in an English-speaking country but since I was deprived a formal education, I had to learn English from English records. I would listen to these records over and over again. My knowledge of English is what helped me to get into nursing school in Uganda at the age of sixteen years. In fact, learning English "took the lid off of the jar" for me and has allowed me to fulfill my life dreams. So, I knew that if I were to reach my potential in the United States, it would be important for me to make sure at some point that my English was the best it could be.

In the fall of 1981, which was two years after I arrived in the United States, I decided to take prerequisite courses—biology and chemistry—at the Greater Hartford Community College (now the Capital Community College in Hartford) for their nursing training program. I also took courses in English and math as well. I was hoping to join the nursing school, but unfortunately I failed to make the appropriate grade in chemistry. However, I was not discouraged. To improve my interviewing skills, I took a course in job-interviewing skills at the Hartford College for Women in the early 1980s as well. This course in particular proved to be extremely helpful. It was as if I felt uneasy or incomplete if I was not learning in a classroom setting. So, in the fall of 1981, and throughout the 1982 and 1983 academic school years, I took a total of five additional courses from St. Joseph College in West Hartford, Connecticut, including a writing class and a psychology class. However, since I had no physical academic records from Uganda of having received a formal education, it was difficult to get into a "real" degree program. I remember one academic institution informing me that since I had no high-school diploma, I could submit my General Educational Development (GED) certificate; but without it, my application would not be considered for admission in most U.S. colleges and universities. Of course, I had no such certificate. But in order to get where I wanted to go, I had no choice but to get my GED certificate. So, what did I do to facilitate this process? I went and approached the principal at a nearby high school, Newington High School, requesting permission to enroll in the adult evening classes with the intent of taking the GED examination. Nine months later, I sat for the exam, and guess what? I passed it and a GED certificate was issued to me in 1984. I was very excited about having crossed this hurdle. And in the spring of 1986, I enrolled in the Greater Hartford Community College's nursing aide training and home health aide programs. I again took night courses as an adult learner. I successfully completed the requirements for both programs, so I was awarded a certificate from each program. These certificates gave me the green light to work as a caregiver for the elderly, the sick, and the disabled. I was now able to get work assignments on a regular basis. While growing up, caregiving was my second major desire in my life after getting married. However, as a caregiver, I had more control in determining whether I would be successful. I wanted to care for human beings who were infirm, elderly, and too young to take care of themselves. To me, the acquisition of these certificates was evidence that God was again rewarding me with His blessings, and I praised His name for it.

It did not take long before I had obtained very good work references from my clients, their families, and my supervisors. Dr. Jan Johnston, a pediatrician by profession, was my supervisor when I was taking care of her mother-in-law, Mrs. Helen Johnston, in Newington, Connecticut, in 1980. Mrs. Helen Johnston was my first client in the United States, and I worked with her for more than three years. One day in a conversation, Dr. Johnston not only suggested, but also recommended, that I enroll in the gerontology certificate program at St. Joseph College. She explained to me how such a certification would not only allow me to get better-paying assignments, but provide me with greater expertise in my chosen career. So, in 1987, I finally took Dr. Johnston's advice and I applied to St. Joseph College's gerontology certification program. Guess what? I was accepted for admission. While a student at St. Joseph College, I took a variety of courses related to working with older people, which was now my main interest and focus. It took me longer to graduate because I could only take a course or class whenever I could afford to pay tuition fees. So, I took courses in the spring of 1987, fall/spring of 1987/1988, fall of 1988, and the summers of 1988/1989 and 1989/1990. This had been the same situation at the other educational institutions I had previously attended. It was difficult, but I was so determined to make it work out. At times, I maintained two jobs to support myself and to pay for my education as well as trying to send money to the foster children I was still helping in Uganda. I would also choose to live with family or a client, which allowed me to save more money for school.

In 1988, after a year at St. Joseph College, I was awarded a small scholarship to be used toward my tuition fees. I was so grateful. A fellow student in one of my gerontology courses, Regina Brananden, was my supervisor at the Every Heights Nursing Home. After only a few class meetings, Regina whispered to me, "Faith, are you sure we are attending the right class?" This class and other classes in the program covered all aspects of aging, including the changes that occur in the body and the mind as we age. The required and suggested readings were interesting and informative, but at the same time scary because we both were within that same age range, sixty-plus. Yes, we were members of the same age groups that we were studying. Unfortunately, my supervisor never attended the class from that day onward. I pressed on because I was determined to increase my knowledge in the field and to make myself more marketable. So, I continued to follow Dr. Jan Johnston's advice to me, but now I pursued my studies with a greater determination.

While at St. Joseph College, I studied very hard and I was happy to discover that all of my tireless efforts had not gone unnoticed. To my joy, I was informed that I had been nominated to receive the 1989 American Outstanding Adult Learner Award. One of my supporting letters came from Marilyn Nielsen, R.S.M., Ed.D., the director of a weekend college I had attended. She wrote such a wonderful letter. In the very first paragraph, she stated, "I believe that Faith Mulira is an exemplary human being who has fought for an education, and more than ever, she is an outstanding adult learner. In spite of being deprived of an education for so many years, she has become educated and maintains a wholesome attitude toward life." I was honored by her words and I waited anxiously for the final selection decision.

I was so elated and proud of myself when the news came that I had been selected as a recipient. So, I, Faith Alexandra Kamya Nasolo Mulira, was awarded a Certificate of Merit as a 1989 Outstanding Adult Learner from the U.S. Department of Education in Washington, D.C. Such an achievement and recognition encouraged me to stay in school and to complete my studies. And, on my graduation day in 1990, I was so happy to receive my hard-earned certificate in gerontology at the age of sixty-six. It was as if that season of my life had been crowned with my certification in gerontology. I had really enjoyed my coursework and the associated research assignments. My fieldwork had put me in contact with some wonderful people, many of who were my clients. I would often-times, with their permission, use my clients and my experiences with them as material and topics for my research papers. In the end, I was able to learn so much from my elderly clients as well as from my teachers and tutors, who usually liked my papers. My teachers and tutors also never failed to give me great comments and wonderful feedback, which helped me to become a better expert in my field. I consider all of my acquired knowledge as a blessing that helped to make me an outstanding caregiver, and I am so grateful.

Another milestone in my life in the United States had taken place on March 11, 1988, when I was honored with U.S. citizenship four months before my sixty-fourth birthday. I was now a bona fide citizen of the United States of America. I was so thrilled. This was indeed a great honor that was bestowed on me, and one of the highlights of my life. With my U.S. citizenship and my certificate in gerontology, I found it easier to get employment assignments. Over the years, my profession as a caregiver has put me in contact with many highly educated people, and I have learned from their life stories and they have learned from mine. I have always taken great pride in taking the best care of my clients. The positive relationships and satisfying encounters I have had with most of them has helped me to go beyond the sadness of some childhood experiences, including the fact that I had missed out on a formal education when my six sisters were provided that privilege. Looking back, I am so proud that I did not succumb to what was culturally expected of me. Throughout my career, I have been blessed because my clients and their families have trusted and appreciated me for taking care of their love ones. I have included four sample letters of recommendation written by the relatives of clients that I have taken care of over the years that highlight not only their gratitude but also my expertise as a caregiver.

LETTER #1: LETTER FROM THE FAMILY OF ANNE MALLEY

January 23, 2002
From: Patricia M. Pye, R.N., B.S.N., and M.S.
RE: Faith Mulira
To Whom It May Concern,

It is with pleasure to write in enthusiastic support of Faith Mulira. Faith is a dedicated professional endowed with special skills. She was employed by my family to take care of my mother during her last years. Mother passed away in October of 2000 at the age of ninety-four.

As an experienced hospital administrator, I can say without hesitation that Faith delivered care with sensitivity in an efficient and effective manner. Her passion for excellence and commitment to high ideals is exceeded only by her genuine love and concern for others. She combines professionalism with compassion, knowledge with skill, and initiative with creativity.

As a family, we will be forever grateful for her patient, caring, warmth, love, and laughter. As a health care professional, I truly believed that she is a role model and catalyst for positive change. Her ability to deal with myriad responsibilities reflects the physical, intellectual and emotional requisites necessary to perform as an outstanding nursing assistant/home health aide.

LETTER #2: LETTER FROM THE FAMILY OF MRS. SELMA

July 22, 2002
From: Carol
RE: Faith Mulira
To Whom It May Concern,

In late 2001, my mother, Selma, age ninety, entered The Manor Nursing Home in Connecticut. She passed away during the first quarter of 2002, with her faculties fairly intact. In addition to Manor staff, my siblings and I hired Faith Mulira to attend to Mother. The level of Mother's care improved greatly with Faith's fairly constant presence at the Manor. Mother trusted Faith, absolutely, and Mother was a very skeptical woman.

I consider as a gift the level of care—both physical and emotional—which Faith Mulira gave Mother during the last few months of her life. Many factors contribute to my views regarding Faith, including her meaningful nursing background, recognition of the dignity of all people (patients, family members, professionals, and nonprofessionals at The Manor), and her integration in the faith community (although not Mother's church) where she is well-respected.

In addition, Faith wisely maintained updated certification as a nurse's aide with the State of Connecticut, enabling her to quickly win over even skeptical management of The Manor when we wanted my mom to have that "extra" care in her failing days. Faith won the hearts and minds of so many people in The Manor and in Mother's hometown area. Their loss is a gain for her New Georgia community that she has moved to.

I highly commend Faith Mulira for her professionalism, her compassion, and her dedication as a member of the caring community.

Please do not hesitate to contact me if you have any questions.

LETTER #3: LETTER FROM THE FAMILY OF MRS. WATKINS

May 11, 2006
From: Mrs. Martha Sue Watkins
RE: Faith Mulira
To Whom It May Concern,

I am writing this letter of reference for Faith Mulira. My husband and I had the good fortune to have Faith come into our lives when we were faced with a requirement of 24/7 in-home care for his mom. Her requirements had finally succeeded what his dad could provide. Faith provided excellent care for Mrs. Watkins who had limited capacity. She was not mobile. She could not provide any personal care. With a loving heart, Faith did everything for her. She prepared all the meals (an excellent cook) for both parents and also light housekeeping. We were very sad when Faith was led to return to Uganda on an important mission; however, because of Faith's integrity and commitment to mom, before she left, she brought us her replacement. She trained her and wrote out detailed instructions for the daily care and medication routines.

Mom was under hospice care. Hospice provided baths five days a week and a nurse came once a week to evaluate conditions. Hospice was very complimentary of Faith and her caregiving skills.

From a short-term illness, we lost dad in March last year; mom followed within three weeks. Had either of them lived and Faith was here, you can be sure that she would be working with us! She is a wonderful lady with a level of caring not often found. In her absence, we experienced many caregivers, so we feel that we are quite able to make that judgment.

You are welcomed to call us if you have any specific questions.

LETTER #4: LETTER FROM THE FAMILY OF MRS. BETTY WHALEY

August 22, 2007
From: Denise Nesper
RE: Faith Mulira
To Whom It May Concern,

My name is Denise Nesper and I had the opportunity to meet, interview, and get to know Faith Mulira in February of this year. My mother, Betty Whaley, had her fourth surgery in three years in February of this year. Each surgery was followed by a lengthy recovery time at home, which necessitated in-home, round-the-clock care for her for about a month. Every care provider assigned to my mother came with a different experience, some okay and some not so good. That is, until Faith came to care for my mom.

It is with great pleasure and confidence that I write to tell you what an excellent, professional care provider Faith is. After the first three surgeries, I myself would stay in the home for up to a week to instruct the care providers and make sure my mother would be well taken care of. After spending less than two days in the home with my mother and Faith, both my husband and I felt confident enough to leave. Faith needed very little instruction. She was extremely attentive to my mother's physical and emotional needs, took no changes, followed instructions in detail, and worked hard to keep order in the house, all with a caring and kind attitude. We couldn't have been blessed with a better caregiver. It is clear to me she has quite a gift for this profession. Faith was also required to stay with my mother for weeks on end, without time off. She also did this with a smile on her face and a great attitude.

If my mother has another surgery in the future, I wouldn't hesitate to call on Faith again. Please feel free to call me any time with specific questions. Faith is a very special woman and I would love to see her employed by someone who will value her gifts and compensate her accordingly.

To provide my clients with the best care, I made a point of taking refresher courses and attending workshops to remain current in my field. I have also tried to remain open to learn new things that were not directly related to my field, but provided me with skills that might indirectly make me more marketable. For example, as early as 2001, at the age of seventy-six, I started classes at a local library to learn how to use the computer. I wanted to be able to better fit in with the computer generation. So, I continue, no matter what part of the world I am in, to learn new things and to acquire new skills. This is one of the many benefits of living in a more industrialized part of the world where there is always an abundance of opportunities. You just have to be brave enough and have some self-confidence and an adventurous spirit to seek them out. Even as recent as the summer of 2010, while staying with my daughter Sanyu in Florida, who lives in a retirement community, I took an oil-painting class that was offered to the community's residents. Being active helps to keep the mind from becoming lazy and aging too quickly. I am so grateful to God who has sustained me through my long journey to be educated. This journey has made me who I am and it has dictated how I relate to others. I only wish that my father and mothers were still alive today to celebrate my accomplishments with me.

Chapter 22

WE WERE SIX; NOW WE ARE FIVE

One of the most devastating of my life losses was that of my only beloved son, Michael Sansa Mulira, who passed away too soon, on April 15, 2008. He was only fifty-eight years old. Michael, born on November 19, 1949, joined his sisters in the United States in 1974 after graduating from law school at Makerere University. Unfortunately, he had to leave the country because of the political situation before obtaining his law license. He lived in Connecticut for a short time and worked for the state of Connecticut before going out on his own. He relocated to Los Angeles, California, where he did paralegal work, developed legal software, and did legal research for very prestigious law firms. To refresh his legal skills, he took some law courses at the University of Southern California in Los Angeles, California. After some time, he became a born-again Christian and joined Crenshaw Christian Center under Apostle Dr. K. C. Price. This blessed change in Michael's life saved not only his soul, but his earthly life as well, because it provided him with the tools to overcome the challenges of alcohol abuse. With the alcoholic abuse taken care of, he was able to become a fully functional and respectable person in the business world. Unlike his father, he had access to Alcoholic Anonymous (AA) and its recovery programs. Michael embraced AA with a passion. Shortly after his deliverance from alcoholism, he met, in 1983, an equally respectable and talented lady. They were married in Los Angeles in November of the following year and, shortly after the wedding, they moved to Sacramento, California. On March 28, 1989, their lovely daughter, Sanyu Ruth Kentugga Mulira, was born. She was named after my oldest daughter Sanyu, which means "joy and peace," and her mother, whose middle name is Ruth.

After living in the United States for some twenty years, Michael returned to Uganda to visit, leaving his wife and daughter, who was then five years old, in Sacramento. This decision forever changed his relationship with his family. He and his wife later divorced; Michael continued to live in Uganda, desiring to be of service to his beloved mother country. Michael went on to establish another family in Uganda and had two other children, Tendo, who was born in 2005, and Kukkiriza, who was born soon after Michael's passing in 2008. However, Michael, like my father, had already chosen the name "Kukkiriza" to be given to the unborn baby in case the baby was a boy child. The name means "faith."

In the summer of 2005, Michael's ex-wife brought their daughter, who was then sixteen years old, to visit her father and to meet her Baganda extended family. It was during this visit that the Muliras came together at an organized luncheon to bestow upon Sanyu her royal name, Kentugga, from the Kingdom of Kooki, in keeping with her father's original roots signified by his middle name, Sansa. Sanyu now became Sanyu Ruth Kentugga Mulira. The name was given to her by the eldest sister of Mike's father, Aunt Ezesa Makumbi, who is well-known in her own right. She was the first and only female member of the LEGICO—Legislative Council in Uganda—in 1960 and 1961 during the period of British colonialism. Furthermore, she was one of the first, if not *the* first, African female member of the Parliament in East Africa. Moreover, for a time, she also worked as a professional actress and starred in the 1948 movie *Men of Two Worlds*. So, it was indeed an honor for Sanyu to be given her traditional royal name by this paternal great-aunt. It was a beautiful luncheon held at the Mulira House in Kampala, which houses the Muliras' historical photographs and other historical artifacts (see Figure 40). And more importantly, this reunion of the father and daughter after some ten years was a blessing to both.

During this particular time, I was actually living and working in Georgia, but visiting Uganda as often as I could because I still wanted to be a contributor to my mother country. I wanted to find a way to help the poor and destitute with some kind of medical services. Also in 2006, Michael fell ill, so I returned to Uganda to help take care of him. The following is a part of the letter he wrote and gave to me as I was leaving to return to Georgia:

> Maama your coming to visit me contributed greatly to my getting better. I was so sick as you realized! I was also worried as to how I was going to handle my medical bills for I needed to see the doctors for treatment. Fortunately, Dr. Dar'Bella returned to Uganda *just in the neck* [*sic*] *of time* to stay, just in time because I needed a good doctor to take care of me. At my last visit to him, he generously offered medical services "free" each time I find myself in need of his services!! Not only once, not twice but anytime I feel a need for his services.
>
> You too, Maama came so unexpectedly soon after Dr. Dar'Bella. It was all God's planning. During the past two months we have shared time together—talking and laughing like we have not done in a very long time. I know that somehow this was divinely ordered by God that we have this time together. I also enjoyed the daily meals that you especially prepared for me and sent to my home. I had been put on a special, no salt diet and you and only you knew how to prepare the delicious dishes that were so satisfying.
>
> Maama, I want to thank you for all of your love, concern and support that you have given and shown me for as long as I have been on this planet. You have always shown endless love for me and have been able to forgive many of my misguided actions. I know that our relationship at times was tested but you always were there for me to lean on and you helped me get up and get going again and again. And for that, I will forever be grateful. I feel especially blessed that you are my mother. Your visit to Uganda at this time is truly a gift from God and I want to wish you a safe and blessed trip back to America.
>
> Your loving son,
> Michael

Before passing away in 2008, Michael had spent some twelve years in Uganda working in different capacities as a legal-software consultant. Even though his career plans to establish an internationally based computer/legal-software business were never brought to full fruition, I truly believe that in my son's heart, his return to his motherland provided him a level of comfort. His legacy will live on through his children, who I daily pray will fulfill their life objectives and dreams while staying close to Christ. Perhaps his most important life contribution besides his three children was the part and key role that he played in developing the business plan and dissecting the project vision for the Masooli Health Care Centre, now renamed the Faith Mulira Health Care Centre.

He completed this fantastic plan in 2007. I thought it was befitting to include part of his business plan as the introduction to this book.

The following letter provides insight into the personality of my son:

Figure 27: My son, Michael Sansa Mulira (1949–2008).

LETTER #1: A TRIBUTE TO MICHAEL MULIRA

It has been an honor to meet and know Michael since our first visit to Uganda almost three years ago. We got to know each other well and formed a real bond. When we returned in 2007, although Michael was in struggling health, he radiated his desire to help us by writing our Business Plan. His gift of creativity, prolific verbal skills, along with an understanding of the United States businessman, made Michael the logical one to relay the dreams and passion of the Faith Health Care Center. The result was a superb Business Plan as was shared by those who read it.

I shall personally miss hearing Michael's reassuring and sincere voice as he greeted us with a true desire to make us feel welcome.

Michael, your struggle is over as you return to our Lord's home triumphantly. May God hold you in his loving arms till we meet again.

Your friend,
Gordon Crouch,
Chair, Faith Mulira Health Care Center Inc. (U.S. Board)

Chapter 23

MY VISION AND MISSION FROM GOD

Since I travel back and forth to Africa, I continue to hold membership in certain organizations in Uganda, including the Mother's Union. It's because of this effort and my desire to maintain a sense of community with and to make a concrete contribution to my mother country that I embarked on the idea of the Masooli Health Care Centre Project. Back in the late 1960s, I purchased five acres of vacant land that was up for sale in the Masooli area. Even though I donated half an acre to be used as a burial site for the family, I had initially purchased the land with the intention of developing it for investment purposes. Unfortunately, I ended up only managing to put up a small neighborhood convenience store with my own funds before fleeing Uganda in 1977. The store had two rooms (each ten feet by ten feet). It was my plan that the money (proceeds) from the shop would be used to help one of the disadvantaged community families to survive in my absence from the country. Initially, one room was to be used for their accommodation and the other for the shop.

One of my long-term goals had always been to return to my mother country and develop my property at Masooli. I loved the area, and I had visited the area very often. In addition, I had made friends with the old and new families in the community. Even though I had no house there, I had started to feel, after purchasing the land, a sense of belonging and a feeling of oneness with the Masooli residents. I also had no ethnic ties with the region, but I immediately developed a burden for the area's inhabitants. And, as I kept visiting the area, I found myself constantly faced with the desperate situation of the people of this community. Most families had very little to live on, yet I saw them have one child after another; as their families grew, the number of unhealthy children roaming around the area also increased. I started to feel a sense of responsibility toward the families in this community. They sought my advice on many issues, and I shared with them all I knew about nutrition, family planning, child and adolescent counseling, and life in general.

After legitimate government was restored in Uganda in the mid-1980s, I made more frequent trips to Uganda. The knowledge I had gained in the sixteen years I worked as an administrator for the first orphanage in the country (SBH), together with my nursing and midwifery training, my diploma in social work, and my experience as a mother, proved to be very useful. I soon realized that the main problem or challenge for the individuals and families I talked with was the same—a lack of knowledge. The people of Masooli, like the people of any community, wanted the best for their families but did not know how to go about it, largely due to their lack of education. They were not lazy. They were hardworking but poor. Instead of seeing the problem as an individual problem, I realized that it was a communitywide problem. And I knew in my heart that I had to do much more if I were to make any meaningful difference in the lives of the people of Masooli Village. It was as if they were looking up to me to help lift them out of their situation.

I knew this feeling too well. All my life, I have had many chances to give back to the community by helping those in extreme need. This is not to say that I had plenty to spare or that I was highly skilled; I was a single mother of five, and raising my children was always a struggle. But God always made a way, and more people kept coming to me for assistance. The assistance I gave was sometimes financial and at other times temporary shelter, or referrals to a contact person, or verbal encouragement to help someone pursue a career. The more I helped others, the more I received from others. I do believe that giving is one of my personal gifts from God.

I also think that this yearn to give and to help others has its beginning in my childhood. As the oldest female child in my family of sixteen, I was denied schooling in order to help my stepmother care for my stepbrothers and stepsisters. While my brothers and later my sisters went through formal school, I was home-schooled by my father. I missed the formal education and social interactions that other children got when they went to school. Even though I managed to get admitted into a nursing training program and later went to the United Kingdom to do a two-year diploma in social work, I always had this feeling that I could have done better in life if I had gotten the chance to go through formal schooling. I have always felt that I had great potential but did not have the opportunity to explore a variety of options. This experience left me with a yearning to do better in life and the belief that sometimes a little help at the right time is all we need to be able to reach our full potential. I was very proud of myself when I finally got my GED in the United States and then went on to college to obtain my gerontology certificate at a very mature age. I would like to add, even though it has been previously stated, the fact that I was also awarded the 1989 "American Outstanding Adult Learners Certificate of Merit" was a monumental achievement for me, as it would be for anyone sixty-four years old.

It is this idea of having potential and not having the opportunity that normally touches my heart to help people in need. I felt that the people of Masooli, especially the children, had potential but no opportunities. This is what led me to abandon my idea of developing the plot of land at Masooli for myself. I thought that I should build a community hall so that the children who had nothing to do to occupy their time would have the opportunity to get together and be taught simple creative activities or games. At the same time, I thought that the adults could be encouraged to attend classes and be taught things they could do to improve their living conditions.

One of the many Masooli cases that really touched my heart was that of two children, a little boy aged six and a little girl aged five, whose father was shot dead in their presence. When I first saw them, they were living in one of the small rooms at my convenience store at Masooli. I was so touched and filled with such heaviness in my heart that I decided that I would always be there for them. Their mother had left them to get remarried. This can often happen in our patrilineal system where a man is reluctant to take on the children from his new wife's previous marriage. According to our tradition, her children belong to the family of the dead husband. However, none of those family members had come to claim these children. So, the two children were fostered with my cousin until they completed high school. By that time, I was living in the United States; since there were no promising opportunities in Uganda, I wanted to bring them to the United States, but at the time I did not have the money.

On one of my return visits to Uganda, I went to Masooli to start clearing the space for the community hall. While I was working, some members of the community approached me and opened up a conversation. They strongly expressed their concern about not having access to health-care services in the area when they were sick. I listened to their endless stories of having to travel too far for health services, and not being able to afford the transportation or the medical treatment they received at these centers. Their children were dying unattended due to these problems. These stories deeply touched my heart and as they talked on and on about the grave need for a clinic in the area, I would at times feel overwhelmed.

So in 1999, I had one of the two rooms at the convenience store converted into a family drug store, which also doubled as a clinic for the Masooli community. I do admit that this was a temporary makeshift clinic and included only the most basic of equipment, which included one bare wood patient-examining table. A visiting doctor would service the patients who came to the clinic, and the visiting doctor usually found a long line of patients waiting to consult with him or her. So, it was more of a place where villagers could pick up over-the-counter medicines than a medical clinic. There were little to no provisions available to treat infectious diseases or obtain any necessary preventive-care services. I was always grieved by this situation, and I wanted to do more for the people of Masooli. So, as the population increased, it became evident that the community needed much more than an informal clinic. Furthermore, many of the residents could not even afford the simple drugs available at this makeshift medical center, which also served as a convenience store and a residence.

As referenced in previous paragraphs, Masooli is a very impoverished community situated less than nine miles from Kampala. Masooli Village is one of nine parishes comprised within the subcounty of the Wakiso District. The entire area is lacking in adequate public transportation, shopping centers, and accessible and dependable medical services. This means, in reference to the latter, that this community, especially its children, are dying unnecessarily due to the absence of the most basic of medical treatments and the lack of health education. Even today in 2010, the main causes of death continue to be linked to communicable diseases that could be prevented through the proper health interventions. I realized that I had to find a way to improve the lot of the nine to ten thousand residents of Masooli Village. So, I began to pray and to ask God to provide me with a clear vision and the means to find others who would support my vision and assist me in making it a reality. When God gives you an assignment, it does not mean that it will be easily completed; it simply means that He has His hands on it, and if you continue to be guided by Him, He will provide the people and the means for you to complete your assignment successfully.

Now, the vision did not come all at once. God sometimes has a way of putting people in your path that facilitate the clarity of your vision or destiny. And I was fully persuaded that Masooli needed a health-care center where the people could not only get medical attention but be taught about preventive care as well. I lacked the funds and the knowledge of how to make this happen, but I felt I had to do whatever I could until I acquired this needed information. So, in the meanwhile, I started collecting used clothing, powdered milk, and other food items, which I would ship in parcels to help these poor people in Uganda. I did this for many years until I could no longer pay for the shipping charges. I also received occasional financial support from the Sunday school at the Congregational Church in West Hartford, Connecticut. Its members helped to pay for the shipping of parcels of clothing, food, and general supplies to the needy in Uganda. On one of my many return visits to Uganda, I started to meet with friends and relatives so that I could share with them what I considered to be my assignment from God. To God be the glory, because many of them agreed that there was a serious need for a professional clinic to be built in the Masooli community. I started also to share the vision with some of my friends in the United States, and as I continued to share it, the vision emerged more clearly.

I spent most of my first fifteen years in the United States in Connecticut because my children all lived in the state of Connecticut. I occasionally attended the First Church of Christ, under the leadership of Reverend Bob Naylor, in Simsbury, Connecticut. I would also see him whenever he visited some of his housebound members who were also my clients/patients. It was the women's group from this church that assisted me with the financial support to obtain the visas for the two children who were being fostered by my cousin after being deserted by their mother. There were no opportunities for them after high school in Uganda, so I was determined to bring them to the United States. As late at 2003, the young girl was in the U.S. Army and the young man was being trained in banking. They are now earnest contributors to the American society.

One Sunday morning soon after the beginning of the twenty-first century, Reverend Naylor asked me what I planned to do when I retire. I immediately replied that I wanted to return to Uganda and try to help my fellow citizens in the Masooli community. I explained how I wanted to help them improve their health conditions by providing them with the badly needed health-care services, inclusive of preventive-care information. I explained to him my heartfelt desire with all of the passion I felt. I also shared with Reverend Naylor the endless cry from the residents of Masooli for health-care services in general and affordable ones in particular. His response was an answer to my prayers. He said that he would work hard to try to raise funds to enable us to put up a facility to meet the needs of the people in Masooli Village. He also told me that it would be built in my memory as a gift from the people for whom I cared for here in the United States. In this way, it would be able to continue to provide services to the people of Masooli for many years after I had gone to be with the Lord. I was so thrilled and amazed, but I still was not sure that I had heard him correctly. We never can be sure how God will bring his assignments into fruition. Reverend Naylor assured me that he meant to help with the fund-raising and that the project was possible. Reverend Naylor then asked if I could find a suitable property site that could be purchased on which to build the clinic. At that point, I informed him that I had a piece of land that I would donate for the purpose of building the clinic in Masooli and that my land donation would be my contribution to the project. So, I donated half of an acre of my land in Masooli for the project.

Reverend Naylor was so pleased that he suggested that I go see Reverend Johnson of the Bethel African Methodist Church in Bloomfield, Connecticut. (I also mentioned Reverend Johnson in Chapter 19 of this book with regard to my healing from breast cancer). Reverend Naylor thought that Reverend Johnson would have the necessary information about managing such a project in Africa. God is so wonderful; I already knew Reverend Johnson. Reverend Naylor was being transferred to another church in Greenwich, Connecticut, so he also suggested that I get in touch with Dr. Gordon Crouch and his wife, Nancy, who would act as his representatives. It was from this point that Dr. and Mrs. Crouch, along with other friends from both churches, formed the U.S. board of directors for the project. The members of this board, under the direction of Dr. and Mrs. Couch, have worked hard to raise funds in the United States to support the project in Masooli. A Ugandan board of directors was also formed to manage the onsite construction details and operations planning, and Professor William Senteza-Kajubi was elected as the chair. Also, the Ugandan board was designed to work very closely with the U.S. board of directors. The facility has been built on the half-acre of land that I donated. We plan to have a preliminary opening ceremony this December and a formal grand opening ceremony in January of 2011. The road has not been easy, but it has been rewarding, and I have made so many new lifetime friends.

Figure 28: The Faith Mulira Health Care Centre, 2008.

I would like to end this chapter with an article written by my late son's only daughter Sanyu, because it not only provides additional insight into my life's work but also validates why the Masooli Project is so important to me. Sanyu, like her father, has the gift of the pen. Her article, entitled "Daughter of Masooli: My Grandmother,

Faith Mulira" was originally published in the "Faith Mulira Health Care Center Newsletter" (Summer 2010, volume 1, issue 2). The article can be found at www.masooliproject/org.

She writes:

My grandmother, Faith Nasolo Mulira, is one of the most phenomenal women I have ever met. She is a loving, caring, and wonderful grandmother, and the passionate affection that she graces upon her family, she also selflessly sheds upon everyone she meets.

At an early age, my Grandma Faith decided that she would take charge of her life and achieve as much as possible, even in the face of great adversities. She has devoted her life to helping people within her chosen profession as a nurse. And in her everyday life, she nurtures, supports and aids all that cross her path.

The pinnacle of my grandmother's devotion to helping people is her Masooli Health Care Centre. For as long as I can remember, my grandmother has wanted to establish a Health Care Centre that would serve and aid people for decades to come. From all the stories that she has told me over the years, the time that she spent running Sanyu Babies Home (an orphanage in Kampala, Uganda and my namesake) was the happiest and most gratifying time of her life.

Sanyu Babies Home was not only her place of work but it was truly her home, and all the children in it were her babies. I believe she felt most true to herself when she was running Sanyu Babies Home because she was at the full disposal of those for whom she was caring. I also believe that the Faith Mulira Health Care Centre at Masooli holds a similar place in my grandmother's heart.

Luckily, about five years ago when I was sixteen years old, I had the chance to not only visit the site of the Masooli Health Care Centre with my grandmother but to witness the enormous pride and hope that filled her as she walked around the grounds. For her, health care is something that everyone has a right to. All people fall ill sometime in their lives, and if there is the potential for treatment of their ailment, they are deserving of it because they are all human beings.

Within the Masooli area and in Uganda as a whole, many people are plagued by preventable and treatable ailments but have nowhere to turn for help. My grandmother's life work has been to provide those in need with viable and affordable health care. Over the years, she has shown her love and commitment to others in the remote hospitals she has worked as well as in her work with children in orphanages.

The Faith Mulira Health Care Centre at Masooli represents my grandmother's more than sixty years of work on behalf of others. I admire Faith not just as my grandmother, but as an amazing woman with the biggest heart I have ever seen.

Sanyu Ruth Kentugga Mulira, 2010

Chapter 24

BATHING IN THEIR APPRECIATION

I am so thankful that my children and I have always been close. It was tough being a single mother. In fact, at times, it was overwhelming. But my children have been my special treasure, and they made my life worth living in the worst of times. I have always remained grateful to God for them and, through them, my most precious grandchildren. Our experiences together have been both sweet and bitter. I do believe that I have had a very positive impact on all of my children and grandchildren. I have also felt appreciated by them and an inspiration to them. All of them have pursued a higher education, or else they are in the process or not yet old enough to do so. For example, Kyomugisha is a practicing medical doctor, Dennis Jr. is a bank accountant, Derrick is an entrepreneur, and Kofi is a biotechnologist, while Sanyu, Kirabo, and Kwame are all in college, and Kojo, Nakasi, and Cody are doing well in high school.

I have also felt very loved by my children and their children. On my seventieth birthday, April 7, 1994, my five children gave me a great celebration. My daughter Sanyu wrote the announcement program/brochure for the occasion and there were two statements in it of which I especially rejoiced. These two statements also made me feel renewed and blessed. The first statement was on the cover page. It read, "A time to celebrate and give thanks for the birth, life, and future of Faith Nasolo Mulira." The mention of the future meant a lot to me because I had so many things that I knew God still had for me to do. The second cherished statement was found inside of the announcement. It read, "Over the years many have come to know Faith as a woman of quiet resolve, boundless energy, endless love, and uncommon beauty." Wow, I thought, what an honor to be "recognized" by your own while you are still alive! And I thought about my mother and father, who would never be able to share this life victory with me.

A time to celebrate and give thanks for the birth, life and future of

FAITH NASOLO MULIRA

August 7, 1994

Figure 29: Seventieth birthday celebration pamphlet cover.

As part of the weekend activities, we attended with our friends and extended family a thanksgiving service at the Bethel AME Church located in Bloomfield, Connecticut. This service was followed with a reception at my daughter Mabel and her husband Jerome's home in Windsor, Connecticut. It was a grand celebration that was memorialized in a twelve-month calendar with different photos of my children and grandchildren for each month. I have included a copy of the announcement pamphlet cover on this page.

Then, ten years later, in celebration of my eightieth birthday, my daughter, Irene Lwamafa, who lives in Kampala, organized a special birthday party in my honor for Saturday, July 17, 2004. It was held at my home at Port Bell, Luzira, with Lake Victoria in view. I was so excited, and I felt so loved and fortunate. There were so many family members and friends who came for the gala affair. Some of the wording on the invitation was also very encouraging and uplifting. It read, "Please join us for a celebration of the *first* eighty years of the continuing life full of love and wonderfully rich with courage, selfless giving and service for people in many parts of the world." The memories of that day are forever printed in my mind. I was so thrilled that my eightieth birthday was celebrated in the home that I had been determined to build. Wow, what a grand milestone accomplishment.

I have always prized myself with having a loving and nonjudgmental relationship with my children. As I discussed in Chapter 13, my pattern of raising my children changed after I returned from the United Kingdom and as I worked with children at SBH. I realized that they needed to be heard, loved, and allowed to develop a strong positive self-image, especially my four girls, void of any cultural limitations and expectations. So, more at a subconscious than a conscious level, I became more accepting of Westernized styles of raising children that were different from how my father parented my siblings and me. In other words, I began to recognize that they were worthy of open self-expression, if they were respectful. I am not saying that I was a "yes, yes" mother, but I did give them the opportunity to explain themselves within limit. The following letter from my daughter Damali provides insight into my parenting style and some idea of what I expected from my children. Her letter also expresses rules and training patterns that continue to be useful in her adult life.

LETTER #1: DAMALI

My Dearest Mother,

I trust you are doing well and that you enjoyed the Mother's Day yesterday. I just wanted to speak with you on that very special day, to let you know the thoughts about you that I didn't get a chance to tell you often. I love you very much and I am proud of you. You have provided such a good example for us to follow and may God continue to bless you for that. Because of your determination, our lives have turned out for the better and we can never thank you enough. Because of your wisdom, we can also now make better decisions. Because of your love for God, we have also found joy in the Lord. I remember before I accepted Christ, you often used to give him the glory, saying that, "God has done so much for me." You always would say that "Nze Mukama ankoled ebikulu bingi nyo," which means, "The Lord has blessed me greatly." I have heard this so many times from you, and now I am a Christian myself, not only do I understand how important it is to hear such expressions but I also believe that this laid the foundation for us to also appreciate what God had done in our lives as well. Today, I can also say with you that "God has done so much for me and I thank him." "May his name be glorified in heaven and in our lives." The Bible tells us that every knee shall bow and every tongue confess, that Jesus is the LORD.

Mom, we love you very much,
Damali

My daughter Irene also sent me a letter entitled "A Tribute to All Mean Moms". It was an anonymous letter she got from the Internet, so, she did not personally write, but it was great. It talked about the wonderful qualities of mean moms and how they fix their children healthy meals, teach them responsibilities, and provide them with rules and structure so they can develop into mature and responsible adults. According to the letter, mean moms do not let their children date too early and when they do date, they meet the girl or the boy at the door and mean moms always establish an honest relationship with their children because they have their children's best interest at heart. Mean moms also have consequences for disobedient children. The letter ended with a statement that the problem with the world today is that there are not enough mean moms anymore. I so loved this letter because of the lightheartedness of its presentation and the seriousness of its content. Irene sent it to me because she thought I had done a good job rearing her and her siblings. And, she was letting me know that she admired, appreciated and loved me very much. What else can a mean mom ask for?

I have always tried to keep my family close and safe and connected with our extended family. To facilitate this, I have provided assistance to help other members. I have made myself available to listen as well as, to provide material and moral support if possible. I recall many years ago when my five children, all under the age of nine years old, and I were living in the one-room nurses' housing, and one of my sisters and her son came to live with us because they had no other option. We were crowded, but we were family and that is what families are supposed to do: take care of one another. I think that it is essential for one to be generous to those in need and this is especially true when they are family members. I have even gone as far as to approach one of the presidents of Uganda, President Milton Obote, for the release of my brother Douglas from prison. Yes, sometimes you even put yourself in harm's way to save a family member.

I have also tried to have a positive influence on my siblings' children and to relate to them as if they were my own children. It was easier to be there for them when they were young, because now they live all over the world. So, appreciation letters from my nieces and nephews have always given me comfort. Their letters not only reflect and give insight into my character, but they make clear my priorities in life as well as emphasizing the importance of family, even when some family members fall short in their responsibilities. They remind me that I have let the Lord use me to bring some light and joy into someone else's life. Their letters also illustrate the overall positive impact that I have had on their lives. The next four letters or partial letters are from the children of my late brothers, Joseph and Shemmie.

LETTER #1: ELIZABETH, DAUGHTER OF SHEMMIE, WHO LIVES IN NORWAY

30 April 1999

Dear Faith,

Notice that I have cut out the "Auntie"! I hope that it will be clear to you by the time you have read through this letter. I hope by now that all my well brought up and well meaning cousins have done the right thing and written to you and made all the right noises about how terrible, and how they wish you to get better as soon as possible. Notice also that I am typing and not writing this letter in long hand. Typing has become much easier for me than writing. It allows me to wipe out or change what I have written without having to start from the beginning again.

I have, in fact, been writing this letter to you, in my mind, ever since I heard that you had been ill and had undergone cancer treatment. I heard about it around Christmas time. Anyway, Doreen told me then. I have been grieving ever since. Although you have fought and won this battle against a deadly disease, I realize for the first time that you are not infallible. You will not be with us forever. It became really important for me to write this letter to you. But, I have been scared to do so because these are not the things you talk about to someone who has just warded off a killer illness. Yet, I believe that I would expect someone who loved me to be able to say these things to me. So, I am taking the risk because I love you, and trust that you will understand that I have to write this to you and that this is the time to do it.

Do you remember when we were all young? I was a kid then. You were somebody that both my parents held in great esteem. I remember how much the deck was stacked against you. You had a job at Sanyu Babies Home that would have consumed any ordinary person, but you did it, and brought up a family of five children alone, at the same time! You were also there to clean up after your brothers!! You took care of their children!! Even when they had much better means to take care of them themselves, you did it mostly on your own money. Harriet, my mother, used to say to me, if you grow up and resembles [sic] anyone at all you pray to God that it will be Faith. I have never forgotten that. That was when I started watching you very closely. You have no idea how important you have been in my life. Anyway, I have always held you as the person I want to be most like, and I think, to some degree, I am managing: I care about people, like you showed me. I *feel* things like you taught me. I am not Unfeeling like so many of our relatives. I don't lie to myself about myself, another thing you taught me.

I learnt integrity, love, caring and humour in adversity from you. I use these things every day and I reach a lot of people because of these values that you gave me.

Then, we all grew up, and became older. You continued to care for everyone. You are the only one who can claim credit for bringing us all together. The Kibukamusokes-Muliras would have never had any contact between them if they didn't have you as their reference point. Despite the distance, there is between you and most of us, geographically, you have a presence in all our lives which none of us can deny. Even those of us you may be angry with and who may be angry with you, know that you were the one who came to take care of my father, Eva, and Paul. So, Faith I wanted to tell you, while I still have the chance, how much I owe you for my life. You have been an extraordinary mentor and friend to me. I have become quite a fine woman because I was blessed with an extraordinary Aunt. Now, we are both old ladies! But, I still admire the woman you are. I no longer need an aunt, but I want you, for the rest of our lives, to think of me as your very closest friend Faith, because I love you *unconditionally*. You can always trust that. Even if I am not in contact for a long time, or at the right times, you are never far from my thoughts.

With all my love,
Elizabeth

LETTER #2: JUNE, DAUGHTER OF SHEMMIE

Dear Aunt Faith,
I love you so-o-o-o-o-so much … It is because of you that I am the kind of person I am today. You've always been the chain link that brings our family together. You always go an extra mile to help whoever is in need. Thank you, thank you, and thank you for being there for us. I am glad to have you as my Aunt. May you be Blessed abundantly … I love you very very much …

June

LETTER #3: MABEL, DAUGHTER OF JOSEPH

My dearest Aunt Faith,
Greetings from all of us … We think [*sic*] a lot about you. We talk about your love and the endless care you render to all of us always … I can never thank you enough for all that you did for me when I was little and for what you are still doing, in kindness, not only for me but for many of us. And, for this I know from the bottom of my heart that had it not been for you and my mom, I wouldn't be where I am today. For that I pray that God Bless you today, tomorrow and forever. Thank you for loving us.

I love you,
Mabel

LETTER #4: DOROTHY, DAUGHTER OF JOSEPH

My dearest Aunt Faith,
I am praying hard to God to give me peace in my heart and to keep your light burning, because it is the only link remaining for our family. You know a chain is made up of pieces clinking into each other and I believe families must be like that. Our family, right from the start had only "one big hook" and that was "You" until

now … I just wonder what type of food did they fed you which was different from all of the others … Thank you for what you are doing for our family, and thank you for loving "Us" always. May God Bless You for who you are …

Your Niece,
Dorothy

These letters from my nieces made me speechless. To be viewed as the person who managed to hold the Kibukamusoke family together is ironic in many ways. I was the one who was generally not expected to be more than a housewife. I was the one who was ridiculed for choosing to be a single mother by leaving her alcoholic husband and for having "too many high expectations" for her children. I was the one without a formal elementary and secondary education. This respect from my nieces is evidence that God decides whom he will raise up. God has rewarded me with his blessings and I will continuously and forever praise Him.

This next letter is from the granddaughter of my former husband's sister. Her name is Deborah and she refers to herself as my grandchild and I accept her as my granddaughter. *Jajja* means "grandmother" in Luganda.

Dearest Jajja Faith,
This is just a small note to remind you that you are a "STAR" and to thank you for being a role model to so many of us. God Bless You.

Love and Prayers,
Omuzukulu [grandchild], Deborah Kaddu-S.

I have been so honored by these letters. The fact that I was seen as their worthy role model means that God's awesome love and the healing power of prayer were sufficient to rid my heart of any malice and resentment I might have harbored in my heart for those who tried to undermine all of the joys and accomplishments that I have experienced in my life thus far. Such letters also testify that I chose to do what God would have had me to do. I opened my heart to those who needed me and so, I give all of the glory and honor to God who strengthens me.

Most of the time when my kids were growing up, my house was full of children. Some of them were friends of my children, while others were the children of my friends who temporarily needed some parental care or guidance or both. However, there were also those children who were fathered by some of my already married brothers. Since the legal wives of these particular brothers found it difficult to accept these children as a legitimate part of the family, the children were oftentimes denied their rights to stay at the home of their father. Now, of course, this goes against the idea of the extended family and the traditional ways of living. We Africans talk about the extended family with open pride, but how many of us actually embrace its essence? A very insightful book that provides insight into this discussion is *The Official Wife* by Mary Karooro Okurut of Uganda. Interestingly enough, women who reject other children of their husbands are usually motivated by fear, fear that this child or those children are going to either undermine the marriage or take something away that belongs to their own biological children, like a larger inheritance, maybe. So, even though no children have any say in how they are conceived, they are oftentimes blamed for their own conceptions and births.

There are times when the father will decide to take care of his children outside of his legal marriage without telling his wife. There are other times when the responsibility falls on another family member, like me, who is sensitive to the needs of children because of his or her own life situation. I have always had a place in my heart for children in such a predicament. And as an adult, I have always desired to give them a hand for support and a shoulder to cry on. I know how important it is that they are loved by at least one person and that they know that their coming into this world was neither an accident nor a mistake. They need to know this in order to develop hope and positive self-esteem. Therefore, the children who came to my home were received with a warm parental welcome. How can one even think of sending a relative's child away, least of all resenting them? No; you love them and you try your best to help them become great levelheaded adults. This is our responsibility as human beings and as Christians. It is for these reasons that I appreciate the letters in this chapter and I do think that God is well pleased with me. And I am also grateful to my stepmother Elsie for allowing me to be brought up at her house after my mother was sent away. She made sure that my father did not chase me out of the house. I also thank God for His favor and for never leaving my side.

Last year, I was honored with a letter from the daughter of my most cherished former client, Mrs. Anne Malley, who passed away in 2000. Mrs. Malley is the precious individual who passionately encouraged me to put my life story to print. I will always be grateful for her persistence and her faith in me. It is for this reason that her family has earned a special place in my heart. When I wrote to her daughter Patricia back in 2009, I never expected such a wonderful, detailed response letter. I have included this letter below.

March 3, 2009

Dear Faith,

How wonderful it was to hear from you. You have been in my thoughts so often. I think time and again about what a good nurse you are and how I hope I have emulated you. You clearly are endowed with special qualities— warmth, patience, caring, compassion and so much more. You took such wonderful care of mother and were so comforting to all of us. It is hard to believe that it has been nine years.

Bill and I were saddened to hear about your son. How devastating it is to lose a child. I am sure, however, that he will live on in the legacy of love he left behind. The building looks wonderful and I know before long it will be fulfilling your dreams by managing the healthcare needs of people of Masooli. Faith, only God will know how many lives your vision and hard work will touch. You will be blessed!

We stayed in New Jersey for about a year until Katie had our first granddaughter, Kaylea. That was the impetus for our move to North Carolina. Until last year, when Bill's mother passed away, we had four generations of Pye's [*sic*] in Charlotte, all because Katie struck up a conversation with a seatmate in an airport waiting room that resulted in a job offer and her relocation to Charlotte ten years ago. Katie and Dave now have two wonderful daughters. Kaylea will be ten in August and Kelsey will be seven in June. They live about fifteen minutes from us.

Our son, Kevin, lives with us. A commercial plumbing company has employed him and one day he may take the plumbing certification exam. He is enjoying life in the South. The weather is generally beautiful albeit today there is snow—a rarity.

Betsy who now goes by her official name Elizabeth stayed in Washington DC until three years ago when she returned home to get her Master's degree in business. It is much less expensive living at home. She will graduate in May and will probably head to some place that is more exciting than Charlotte. She has been working with Katie in a children's store and with a disaster relief company. Although she has the two part-time jobs, she spends most of her time studying and using her dad as her chief tutor and editor. She has so many papers to write. She is doing very well.

Bill has retired since we arrived in Charlotte and seems to be busier than ever. He was the president of the Homeowner's association for five years, a babysitter par excellence for our grandchildren, Elizabeth's at home tutor, and took awesome care of his mother until she passed away just before Christmas this year.

I enjoyed retirement for a couple of years. Katie and I did find a part-time job at the children's store where she is now the Manager. After a year, I decided that I missed the hospital and found my current position as Director of Cardiovascular Services for Carolinas Medical Center. It is an 866-bed hospital and I have done things that I have never had the opportunity to do before. I have a great team of people who take pleasure in reaching out to others. They enjoyed doing the bake sale for your healthcare clinic and have passed the word onto others. Hopefully, we will be able to do more. There is a group that, sometime down the line, would love to come to Uganda and offer assistance. A group did go to Ghana last year. What a great trip they had.

Faith, you are a very special person. You have clearly inspired me to be the best nurse I can be. You will be blessed always for the lives you have touched and the love you have shared.

Thanks for a wonderful letter, thanks for all you do!
Patricia

Patricia had written a letter of recommendation for me in 2002; however, this recent response letter was more personal, and it was both gracious toward me and inspirational to me. It does my soul good to know that I inspired her to be the best nurse she could be. It is as if I passed on to her what her mother passed on to me—the drive to do with passion and dedication what we have decided to dedicate our lives to achieving. I am so humbled that she thought of me as someone to emulate. Such professional and personal appreciation not only uplifts my spirit but also is evidence that God's plan in and for my life is being fulfilled.

Chapter 25

A TIME OF ADJUSTMENT, REFLECTION, AND THE FUTURE

Over the years, my children and I have lived happily in the United States. There have been times when we missed our mother country, our close relatives, and members of our extended family, but most of all we have missed that feeling of "belonging" we always had in Africa. However, from the beginning, we were determined to make it work in the United States, to stay put, and make ourselves fit in our new welcoming and sometime not-so-welcoming society. We are grateful and thankful for our new friends and life opportunities. We achieved that oneness of a family that my father tried to teach my siblings and me but did not know how to show us his love and affection. Unfortunately, we all grew up and went our own ways. Some of us maintained close contact over the years, while others lived their lives independently of our extended family. I still think that our father deserved credit for his efforts to create a closely knitted family and for instilling in each of us a desire to succeed in life, educationally and professionally. All of his children received some type of academic degree. To illustrate this, I will provide in the past tense the occupations of all of my siblings, those deceased and those alive. Douglas had a degree in agricultural management and worked for many years for the Ugandan Tea Company and for the Ugandan Hotels; Roscoe was a surveyor; Shemmie, Paul, and Joseph were successful self-employed businessmen; John was a professor of medicine; Rhona was a medical clinical technician at Mulago Hospital; George was in management for the Esso Gas Company; Mary was a certified chartered accountant; Ndiwoza graduated with a degree in education and was a lecturer at Makerere University; David worked for the Ugandan Tea Company; Moses was a medical doctor; Evelyn worked for the United Nations; Florence worked for some universities in Uganda and is now a successful businesswoman; Maria graduated from high school, but I do not remember her profession. Of my fifteen siblings, only six are still alive—Rhona, George, Ndiwoza, David, Evelyn, and Florence. I thank God that my five children knew not only the importance of maintaining close ties with one another, but the importance of remaining a part of each other's lives as if they were a community unto themselves, while still including others.

In all of the states in which I have lived for an extended period of time, including Connecticut, Georgia, California, New York, and most recently Florida, I have tried to become part of that community. Becoming involved in the communities in which I have lived has provided me with a feeling of belonging and with many new friends. I have made a point of joining and regularly attending a local church, and I have participated in church activities like Bible study classes. I have also joined and retained memberships in appropriate professional organizations like the Certified Nurse's Aides (CNAs). I have been a caregiver for the sick and elderly for all of the thirty-plus years I have lived in the United States. I have enjoyed my career, so I still want to be connected. In Connecticut, I was a volunteer member of the National Organization for Social Services, and I also did volunteer work for the American Blood Mobile, Hartford Hospital, and the Jefferson House in Newington, Connecticut. I always made sure to be involved in voluntary community activities because I wanted to be a full member of the communities in which I lived. Even when I visit Uganda, I make a point of giving informational talks at churches and to women's groups.

Having lived in the United States for more than thirty years also means that I have assimilated many aspects of the American lifestyle in the same way that my father underwent certain levels of cultural assimilation of the British culture. It has become very evident to me that my concept of time, many of my food choices, my ways of cooking, the way I relate to my children and grandchildren, my overall way of doing things, my political views as well as my thoughts on the rights of women, to name just a few, have all been culturally influenced by American society. In the United States, I have, at times, exercised the freedom to respond to political or social situations that I think can threaten the social fiber of the society. For example, during the Clinton scandal, I wrote the following letter of support (which was originally handwritten) to First Lady Hillary Clinton in February of 2000, while I was living in Connecticut. I wanted to let her know as a concerned and sympathetic fellow American that she was not alone and that she had my support and my prayers.

LETTER TO THE FORMER FIRST LADY HILLARY CLINTON

February 28, 2000
To Her Excellency
The First Lady Hillary Rodham Clinton
White House, Washington, D.C.
My dear, The First Lady,

For a long time I have wanted to write this letter to you, but never had the courage until now when the Lord gave me the courage to pick up a pen and write.

The main purpose of writing to you Madam is to let you know that my family, my many friends, and myself have failed to find the right words to express our gratefulness to you. You have done quite a lot of nice things for "US" and for the American People at large. More importantly, you stood by your husband, Our President, when he was going through a hard time! We ADMIRE you because you set a wonderful example, (the most wonderful example) to all the women all over the world. Your consideration, tolerance, forgiveness and understanding, proved to us that you are a wonderful Lady! We believe that it was because of "YOU" Madam, that Our Beloved President is still with us as OUR LEADER TODAY! God used YOU to save him for us. We like him a lot. We pray that the LORD BLESS YOU a million times for what you did in the past, for what you are doing today, and for all your endeavors in the future. You proved yourself to be a GREAT OUTSTANDING PERSON!!

Personally, I am an African woman of seventy-five years young, originally from Uganda, East Africa. I came to the United States twenty-one years ago. I am now a United States citizen, a nurse by profession, and a graduate in Gerontology from Saint Joseph College in Connecticut. I have taken care of my fellow senior citizens in their homes for the last twenty years, a career, that I have found very rewarding.

Lady Clinton, I pray that God bless you and yours forever.
Respectfully yours,
Faith Kamya Nasolo Mulira

Yes, I did receive a White House response, and it did not matter to me whether Mrs. Clinton actually typed it herself. However, I was not able to get a publishing release for the letter from the Library of Congress in Washington D.C. Nevertheless, I am very grateful that my letter to her was *not only read but*

Figure 30: Former First Lady Hillary Rodham Clinton's Photograph.

was considered worthy of a response. In her response, she thanked me for my letter, expressed her appreciation for my thoughtful words and mentioned that my support was very meaningful to her. She also encouraged me to continue my support of the Clinton Administration's work on behalf of the American people. Interesting enough, I felt that my voice had been heard. Some years earlier, I had written a letter to First Lady Nancy Reagan, but for a different reason. I was asking her to help me support some needy children in Uganda for whom I had been paying school fees. This was a time when I didn't have a job and could not support them anymore. Mrs. Reagan replied to my request, stating that she couldn't help as she preferred to take care of the needy children who were also in large numbers in America. She wished me well in my pursuit. I also wrote a letter to President Carter requesting his assistance, through programs during his administration that concentrated on renovating housing for the poor worldwide. He wished me well but explained that they could only help provide housing in the areas where there was an organization already set up in the area. There was no Masooli Project at that time. I saw these letters, especially the one to Mrs. Clinton, as an exercise in my First Amendment rights.

I consider myself a very fortunate eighty-six-year-old individual. I have had a long and full life. I am relatively fit, happy, and satisfied with what I have achieved in life, and I am grateful to God for what he has already done for me. In the future, I plan to continue traveling back and forth to Uganda; however, I must admit that those long airplane rides are becoming more strenuous. I have wonderful children, beautiful grandchildren, lovely friends, and great associates. I am very close to God with a consuming love for people, especially those in need. So, when I look to the future, I can only thank the Lord for where I am now and ask Him for grace for the future. I am looking forward to the grand opening of the Faith Mulira Health Care Centre at Masooli. It is such a generous gift by the congregations of several churches and friends in Connecticut. I am so thankful to them for assisting in this gift to the people of Masooli. I am also looking forward in serving as the founding/executive director emeritus of the Centre. I will enjoy providing guidance whenever requested or needed.

I have so many hopes for my twelve grandchildren, who range in ages from two to thirty years old. I am so proud of all of them and I pray for their safety, good health, and overall success in life. I especially pray to God that they learn to make balanced decisions while realizing that they should always keep God close. I truly believe that they are all on the right path. Already, one is an artist, musician, and entrepreneur, one is a medical doctor, another is a biotechnologist, three others are in their final years of college, and I pray that the remaining will follow in the great footsteps of their older cousins.

I have spent many years as somewhat of a lobbyist for the elderly, the sick, and those who are too young to take care of themselves or to speak up for their rights. The most precious of them all have been the children who, for whatever reason, found themselves alone. A child does not ask to be born into this world or into a particular family. So, it is important that parents be careful in how they treat and what they say to a growing child. It is so easy to damage a child emotionally in such a way as to cause the hurt to follow the child until death, if no intervention takes place. I know because it almost happened to me. It is not possible to read a child's mind, nor should we blame a child for being born. A parent should give his or her child love and provide the child with a loving and safe environment in which to grow into a whole individual. When this does not take place, regardless of the reason, the child can develop scars that can last a lifetime. The child can lose his or her life balance. Feelings of unworthiness, rejection, resentment, and sometime a lack of emotions can become embedded in the child's heart.

In my growing-up years, I had both good and bad experiences. Some of the bad experiences left me with painful emotional scars that I have found very difficult to completely erase, and I am eighty-six years old.

For example, my lifetime quest to be educated can be closely linked to the fact that I was denied a formal education, unlike my other fifteen brothers and sisters. At times, I was filled with resentment toward all those individuals I thought had a say in denying me this privilege. I have also had many good experiences which have, along with my many blessings from God, given me the strength to override the painful memories. Today, because God has been so good to me and has always lifted my burdens, I can honestly say that I no longer harbor any grudges in my heart. I am comforted in knowing that I have the respect of many people from all walks of life, and I am happy.

I have tried, especially with my work in Uganda, to aid children who have had their voices taken away. This includes not only the orphans at SBH but also those children whose mothers remarried and then left them to fend for themselves, like the two children I found in my convenience store in Masooli Village. I have helped and cared for hundreds of children who were denied their rights. I, unlike many such children, was fortunate that I was allowed to grow up in a home where my stepmother was kind. She took care of my brothers and me, even before she had children of her own with our father.

I mentioned in a previous chapter how I took painting classes (fabric painting and oil painting) while visiting my daughter Sanyu, who lives in a retirement complex in Florida. I really enjoyed the classes and I found them relaxing and refreshing. I had no idea that I would be so good. My hand especially took to the brush in my scenery paintings. I got so many compliments on all of my paintings from my teachers and my fellow classmates. So, the birthing of these new artistic skills gave me an idea. I thought of the boys and girls in Uganda who had dropped out of school because of their lack of money for school fees. What if they were taught these skills? With this in mind, I began to devote myself to learning how to put beautiful decorations on a variety of fabrics. I decided that if I traveled back to Uganda and was not able to return to the United States for any reason, I would encourage these children to come work with me, painting designs and decorations on T-shirts that could be sold to the public. These young people would learn a skill, as well as earn wages, which in turn would allow them to take charge of their lives. I would be doing something I truly like while helping some of God's treasures, his children in need.

These days, I am so impressed with myself. I do not mean this in a vain sense. I am only acknowledging that I have come so far in accepting my own value and worth. And I recognize my inner strengths, which have their roots in my childhood and young-adulthood. I am so satisfied with my academic and professional achievements, some of which surpass the achievements of those who have had far less obstacles in their lives. I say this not to idly boast, but to show what a person can accomplish even when the odds are not in his or her favor. If you read this book and have had similar childhood experiences, I say, do not despair; God's blessings and grace are sufficient for all of us. At birth, He gave each of us abilities. We must choose to be happy; we must decide to succeed in life; and we need to contribute to the community or communities in which we live. We are all God's children, and He indeed cares for us; we should in turn take care of one another as brothers and sisters. We must decide for ourselves what we are going to do for humanity since God has already given us the tool—the Golden Rule. According to many of my paternal relatives, I was not meant to achieve anything of importance, especially nothing as important as the Faith Mulira Health Care Centre that will one day receive international recognition for the thousands of people it will serve. It feels good to help others, but it feels even better when you help people to help themselves. I hope you enjoyed reading the book. I have added a few more photographs of family members and a photograph of the city of Kampala.

PICTURES OF OTHER FAMILY MEMBERS

Figure 31a: Damali's family, July 2005 (*From bottom to top:* Cody, Kojo, Damali, Kwame, and Kofi).

Figure 31b: Damali and family with husband Kwasi Osei, 1999.

Figure 32a: Dr. Dennis K. W. Lwamafa.

Figure 32b: Irene's family—Irene, Dennis Jr., and Kyomugisha Lwamafa, 2010.

Figure 33: Sanyu Barnicoat and her niece Sanyu in Sacramento.

Figure 34: Sanyu's son Derrick Barnicoat, 1996.

Figure 35: Derrick Barnicoat in 2010.

Figure 36: Michael and Jessie's wedding December 24, 1983.

Figure 37: Sanyu Ruth Kentugga Mulira, 2007.

Figure 38: Me, Sanyu, and Jessie in Sacramento, 2008.

Figure 39: Me, Jessie, Sarah, Sanyu, and Sarah's husband Sam, in Uganda, 2005.

Figure 40: The Mulira House in Kampala, 2005.

Figure 41: Kampala, Uganda, as of today.

CHAPTER QUESTIONS

TOTAL POSSIBLE POINTS 125

TRUE/FALSE, MULTIPLE CHOICE AND FILL-IN QUESTIONS ARE
WORTH ONE POINT EACH. SHORT ANSWERS AND ESSAYS
ARE WORTH TWO TO FIVE POINTS EACH.

CHAPTER 1: QUESTIONS

FILL IN THE BLANK.

1. _____ were always the Kabaka's head rulers stationed in different parts of the Buganda Kingdom.
2. Mr. Festus Mawanda Kibukamusoke attended the _____ High School.
3. _____ is the birth mother of Faith Mulira.
4. The term _____ refers to the wife who is positioned as the leader of the other wives married to her husband.
5. _____ was Faith's stepmother.

CHAPTER 2: QUESTIONS

CIRCLE THE CORRECT RESPONSE.

1. Mr. Festus Kibukamusoke was a perfectionist and a no-nonsense individual. However, he was also very affectionate to his family. True or False

2. Faith's father especially liked the nickname "Festo, the bad guy" because it caused the people with negative intentions to stay away from his children. True or False

3. Mr. Festus Kibukamusoke found it very easy to interact with his African neighbors and the people in the government of the Kabaka because he was an advocate of African nationalism. True or False

4. Mr. Festus Kibukamusoke, being very traditional in his beliefs, made sure that all of the totemic restrictions of his clan were closely observed. True or False

5. The totemic system was originally established to strengthen the relationship of clan members in the area of mutual assistance and, when necessary, defense. However, the system was not designed to regulate the social life of the community, especially where marriages were concerned. True or False

6. Being in a patrilineal structured society, Faith's stepmother had no choice but to follow her husband's rules and decisions. Therefore, Elsie refused to let Yunia see her children once she was sent away. True or False

7. As a minister of the gospel, Faith's father made sure that all of the children had their own individual Bible and prayer book. True or False

8. In Faith's father's house, boys and girls had separate duties. In fact, the boys had to do very little in comparison to the girls. For example, the girls had the sole responsibility of knitting the sweaters for the family. True or False

9. The British liked the company of Faith's father because he preferred the European way of doing things. He even had a government car and driver at his disposal. True or False

10. Briefly discuss Faith's comment about her father with at least two examples, ... "Infact, he behaved and thought more like a British man in a Black man's skin."

CHAPTER 3: QUESTIONS

FILL IN THE BLANK.

1. In _____, King's College Budo accepted the first twelve girls to attend its Primary School, and Faith was one of them.

2. The first Western-type schools in Uganda were established by European missionaries of various denominations. The _____ established both King's College Budo and Gayaza High School.

3. _____ is the site where the cultural coronations of the Kabakas of the Kingdom of Buganda are enthroned in a traditional ceremony.

4. _____, the thirty-fourth Kabaka, who reigned from 1887 to 1939, was the first Kabaka to attend King's College Budo.

5. The term _____ referred to the special "whipping cane" of Faith's father.

6. The present public educational system of Uganda continues to be based on the _____ model.

7. _____ University is still the main university in Uganda.

CHAPTER 4: QUESTIONS

FILL IN THE BLANK OR CIRCLE THE CORRECT RESPONSE.

1. The public education in Uganda was always compulsory even before it was based on the British model. True or False

2. When Faith's oldest brother, Douglas, was nine years old, his father put him out of the house. Douglas lived with his mother for several years in the Buruli District. When he moved back to Kampala, he moved into a Salvation Army mission. True or False

3. _____ enrolled Douglas into his school. Later, Douglas was admitted to both King's College Budo and the University of Makerere.

4. In the immediate years after colonialism, access to a formal education in Uganda was no longer competitive because there were so many private and public institutions of higher learning. True or False

CHAPTER 5: QUESTIONS

FILL IN THE BLANK OR CIRCLE THE CORRECT RESPONSE.

1. Faith entered the Nurses' Training College at Mengo Missionary Hospital in _____, at the age of sixteen.
2. Dr. Jan Johnston, an English female pediatrician, was instrumental in helping Faith get into the NTC. True or False
3. In _____, Faith was accepted into the Midwifery Training College at Mengo Missionary Hospital.
4. In _____, Faith graduated as a certified midwife.

STUDENT'S NAME _____

CHAPTER 6: QUESTIONS

FILL IN THE BLANK OR CIRCLE THE CORRECT RESPONSE.

1. Yona Mukasa Mulira was born on _____.

2. During World War II, when Yona met Faith, he was a lieutenant stationed in England and she was working as a staff nurse at the Mengo Missionary Hospital. True or False

3. Growing up, Faith underwent a traditional initiation ceremony that was designed to teach her the responsibilities of a wife and mother. True or False

4. Before Yona went back to the army, he gave Faith an engagement ring and a beautiful Bible. True or False

CHAPTER 7: QUESTIONS

FILL IN THE BLANK.

1. The **Basuuti**, also called the _____, is the traditional dress style of the women of the Baganda culture.

2. The _____ is the traditional long, white dress shirt for the Baganda men. This shirt is worn over their pants. In addition, the men usually wear a suit jacket with it as well, especially as formal attire.

3. _____ is a Luganda term referring to the practice of giving a bridal price/dowry to the parents of the bride-to-be.

4. The Luganda word _____ refers to a meeting where the groom's relatives officially introduce themselves to the bride's relatives at the bride-to-be's parents' house.

CHAPTER 8: QUESTIONS

CIRCLE THE CORRECT RESPONSE AND RESPOND TO THE SHORT-ANSWER QUESTION.

1. Faith's lady of honor was
    a. Joyce Naylor.
    b. Rebecca Mulira.
    c. Rebecca Kibukamusoke.
    d. Nancy Crouch.
    e. Yunia Mulira.
    f. Gera Mosha.
2. Faith's wedding dress was imported from Kenya. It was a surprise from her fiancé. True or False
3. Briefly discuss at least two reasons why Mrs. B. refused to be Faith's "lady of honor."

CHAPTER 9: QUESTIONS

FILL IN THE BLANK OR CIRCLE THE CORRECT RESPONSE.

1. Faith's wedding ceremony was held at the _____ located in Kampala.
2. The **Akasiki** Celebration takes place a week before the wedding at the bride's home only. True or False
3. On the day of the wedding, Faith's mother was unable to attend because she had fallen ill and had to be rushed to the hospital. True or False
4. One of Faith's brothers-in-law, _____, was the **Gombolola** chief/district subcounty chief, stationed in a town near Jinja.
5. _____ is a green banana that is usually mashed and steamed in a pot over a charcoal stove wrapped in banana leaves when cooked the traditional way.

CHAPTER 10: QUESTIONS

FILL IN THE BLANK OR CIRCLE THE CORRECT RESPONSE.

1. Yona was a prince from the Kingdom of
   a. Ankole.
   b. Iteso.
   c. Kooki.
   d. Bunyoro.
   e. Baganda.

2. By profession, Yona was a surveyor, so he had no trouble finding employment after the honeymoon. True or False

3. From 1950 to 1956, Yona worked in Tanzania as an engineer building local government housing. However, Faith and the children remained in Uganda. True or False

4. Faith, realizing the need to provide a stable income for the family, took a one-year job assignment in the country of _____.

5. _____ is made with maize flour that is meshed into a kind of dough. It is a staple among some ethnic groups in _____.

6. When Faith returned to Uganda in 1957, she went back to work full-time in her field of expertise as a

   _____.

7. According to Faith, she might have been not only the first woman to ride a moped on the streets of Nairobi, but the first female to purchase one in Kenya. True or False

CHAPTER 11: QUESTIONS

FILL IN THE BLANK OR CIRCLE THE CORRECT RESPONSE.

1. Sanyu Babies Home, the oldest orphanage in Uganda, was established in 1929 by the late
   a. Sylvia Gaster.
   b. Milnes Winfred Walker.

2. During the years of the early twentieth century, factors relating to an increase in the number of orphans in Uganda included local traditional beliefs. For example, it was believed by some local cultures that if a woman died in childbirth, the child was the guilty party. True or False

3. In 1958, Faith was hired as the director of Sanyu Babies Home. True or False

4. _____ is considered the pioneer orphan of Sanyu Babies Home and the author of a two-year training program for the nursery's nursing workers.

CHAPTER 12: QUESTIONS

FILL IN THE BLANK OR CIRCLE THE CORRECT RESPONSE, AND RESPOND TO THE SHORT-ANSWER QUESTION.

1. At the age of thirty-eight, Faith was admitted to the _____ in the United Kingdom for a two-year program in social work.

2. Unfortunately, Faith was very unhappy with the two-year program in the United Kingdom because it did not provide any real opportunities to work with different international organizations that emphasized childcare in the United Kingdom. True or False

3. Of all the countries Faith visited in Europe, England was the most familiar. Please discuss why.

CHAPTER 13: QUESTIONS

FILL IN THE BLANK OR CIRCLE THE CORRECT RESPONSE.

1. Faith's UK experience proved to be beneficial in a variety of ways. But more importantly, she learned the importance of providing a home atmosphere that allowed for positive self-development, demonstrative love, and open communication. True or False

2. Faith's Canadian donors requested a meeting with her entire family after she returned to Kampala from the United Kingdom because they were so impressed with Faith's academic achievements. True or False

3. After Faith returned to Kampala from the United Kingdom, her father and paternal relatives were more supportive of her choices and living style. True or False

4. All of Faith's female children attended _____ High School, while her son Michael attended _____.

5. In Uganda, British colonialism lasted from November 18, 1882 to October 9, 1962. True or False

CHAPTER 14: QUESTIONS

FILL IN THE BLANK OR CIRCLE THE CORRECT RESPONSE.

1. Under British colonialism, the policy of _____ meant that the British were going to rule their colony or protectorate through the traditional African rulers. However, the British would maintain control because the African chiefs and kings were answerable to them.

2. Unfortunately, prior to the establishment of British colonialism, Uganda had only two organized kingdoms, Buganda and Bunyoro. True or False

3. In 1964, Faith was appointed the _____ of Sanyu Babies Home.

4. In 1971, Faith received a government scholarship to further her professional development in the United States. So, for this program, she was enrolled as a student at _____ in Ohio.

5. In _____, Faith retired from Sanyu Babies Home after some sixteen years of employment and service.

CHAPTER 15: QUESTIONS

FILL IN THE BLANK OR CIRCLE THE CORRECT RESPONSE.

1. Idi Amin came to power on January 25, 1971, after launching a successful coup against President Yoweri Museveni. True or False

2. It was under President _____ that Faith was able to rescue her brother Douglas from Luzira Prison.

3. In 1975, Faith paid roughly US$240 for three-quarters of an acre of prime land near Lake Victoria. She purchased it from the Kampala City Council for the purpose of constructing her house. True or False

4. _____ was the owner of the airline agency who allowed Faith to pay off her children's airline tickets to the United States on an installment plan.

5. In 1978, Faith's house was completed by her sister-in-law _____.

CHAPTER 16: QUESTIONS

CIRCLE THE CORRECT RESPONSE.

1. As president of Uganda, Obote, a veteran of the British King's African Rifles, was strongly supported in his leadership decisions by the British. True or False

2. When Faith first applied for one of the stores formally owned by an East Indian, she was initially refused. However, once she paid a bribe to the appropriate individual, a store was allotted to her. True or False

3. Faith took out a business loan from the Libyan Arab Bank to renovate and to stock the store she received from the Ugandan government. True or False

4. President Amin was very pleased with the East Indian population in Uganda because of their economic achievements. He even encouraged them to become Ugandan citizens. True or False

5. When Faith left Uganda in 1977, she spent the next years in Kenya working in various hospitals. Once she had earned enough money, she purchased an airline ticket to join her children in Connecticut. True or False

CHAPTER 17: QUESTIONS

CIRCLE THE CORRECT RESPONSE.

1. Faith's mother Yunia, her stepmother Elsie, and her father were all buried in the family burial grounds at Masooli, located some eight miles from Kampala on the Gayaza Road. True or False

2. Near the end of his life, Faith's father reconciled his relationship with all of his sixteen living children. True or False

3. Faith's father was fortunate in his period of retirement to have two pensions, one from the Ugandan government and one from the traditional Buganda government. True or False

4. Briefly discuss how Faith's father responded to the news of the deaths of his wife Yunia and Faith's husband Yona.

CHAPTER 18: QUESTIONS

CIRCLE THE CORRECT RESPONSE AND RESPOND TO THE SHORT-ANSWER QUESTION.

1. When Faith arrived in the United States in 1979, she was astonished that so many everyday Americans were so knowledgeable about Africa. True or False
2. Briefly discuss some of the images of Africa and Africans, held by many Americans, that Faith discovered through her conversations with fellow Americans.

CHAPTER 19: QUESTIONS

CIRCLE THE CORRECT RESPONSE.

1. Faith's father was often called on to give sermons at St. Paul's Cathedral since he also had a degree in divinity. True or False
2. Faith, unlike her siblings, was not baptized until the day that she got married. True or False
3. Many of the early missionary groups in Uganda tried to teach their African converts that all men were God's children. Most of them also went as far as to interact socially with their African converts outside of the church on a regular basis. True or False

CHAPTER 20: QUESTIONS

FILL IN THE BLANK OR CIRCLE THE CORRECT RESPONSE.

1. Faith is a strong believer in healing through the power of prayer. True or False
2. Faith's sister, Evelyn, was seriously hurt in the Ugandan plane crash in Rome in 1989. Faith went to Europe to be of assistance and was instrumental in getting her sister transferred to London, where Faith was able to work as a staff nurse and be close to Evelyn. True or False

CHAPTER 21: QUESTIONS

FILL IN THE BLANK OR CIRCLE THE CORRECT RESPONSE.

1. In _____, Faith received her GED. To do so, she took preparatory classes at the Newington High School in Newington, Connecticut, before taking the test.
2. In _____, Faith enrolled in the Greater Hartford Community College's nursing aide training and home health aide programs. She was eventually awarded a certificate for each program.
3. _____ was Faith's first caregiver client in the United States.
4. Faith was honored with U.S. citizenship on _____, a month before her sixty-fourth birthday.
5. In 1979, Faith chose to come to the United States because
    a. her children were already living in the United States.
    b. she was seeking physical safety in a less conservative society.
    c. she thought the United States would have more occupational opportunities.
    d. All of the above.
6. Faith was accepted into the St. Joseph College Gerontology Certificate Program in _____.
7. In 1989, while at St. Joseph College, Faith received the _____ Award from the U.S. Department of Education in Washington, D.C.

CHAPTER 22: QUESTIONS

FILL IN THE BLANK OR CIRCLE THE CORRECT RESPONSE.

1. Faith's son was once a member of _____ under Apostle Dr. K. C. Price in Los Angeles, California. It was at this church that he was delivered from alcoholism.

2. The names Sansa and Kentugga are royal names from the Kingdom of
    a. Buganda.
    b. Tutsi.
    c. Kooki.
    d. Ankole.
    e. Iteso.

CHAPTER 23: QUESTIONS

FILL IN THE BLANK OR CIRCLE THE CORRECT RESPONSE.

1. Faith Mulira's great-grandparents were once residents of Masooli. In fact, this is the main reason that the people of Masooli were so precious to her. True or False

2. The Faith Mulira Health Centre officially opened its doors to the people of Masooli on November 7, 2008. True or False

3. Reverend Naylor and Pastor Alvan Johnson both went to Uganda to initiate the opening of the Centre. Thousands of people had attended the ribbon-cutting ceremony a week before it opened its door to accept its first patient. The guests were speechless when Reverend Naylor and Pastor Johnson arrived at the ceremony in the van they had purchased for the Centre. True or False

CHAPTER 24: QUESTIONS

FILL IN THE BLANK OR CIRCLE THE CORRECT RESPONSE.

1. To improve and to maintain currency in her professional field, Faith would enroll in courses at various local academic institutions. True or False

2. Faith's seventieth birthday weekend celebration is memorialized in a _____ with different photos of her children and grandchildren.

CHAPTER 25: QUESTION

RESPOND TO THE SHORT-ANSWER QUESTION.

1. Briefly discuss what might be considered Faith's heartfelt mission in life. Provide at least four detailed examples.